Cuckoo

Animal
Series editor: Jonathan Burt

Cuckoo

Cynthia Chris

REAKTION BOOKS

Published by
REAKTION BOOKS LTD
Unit 32, Waterside
44–48 Wharf Road
London N1 7UX, UK
www.reaktionbooks.co.uk

First published 2024
Copyright © Cynthia Chris 2024

Printed and bound in India by Replika Press Pvt. Ltd

A catalogue record for this book is available from the British Library

ISBN 978 1 78914 931 9

Contents

1 What Is a Cuckoo?

how long
to wait for the cuckoo
about a thousand years
Matsuo Bashō, 1672[1]

Pity the common cuckoo (*Cuculus canorus*), a bird on to whom humans have projected some of our most elaborate fantasies. From the utopic, otherworldly city of birds, 'Cloud Cuckoo Land', in Aristophanes' fifth-century BCE comic play *The Birds*, to Sonny, the animated cuckoo who has appeared in advertising campaigns for a General Mills cereal since 1962, the cuckoo embodies moments when fantasy collapses into folly, or when exuberance tilts towards inanity. Consider, too, the umbrage some take at the reproductive strategies of some cuckoo species: Charles Darwin couldn't resist calling their behaviours 'strange and odious'.[2] Science journalist Ed Yong went so far as to call cuckoos 'murderous slackers'.[3] Scottish naturalist James Hardy, writing in the late nineteenth century, took a refreshingly different view, calling the common cuckoo 'this darling bird'.[4] Bethan Roberts, author of *Nightingale* in this very series, struck a more ambivalent stance upon hearing a cuckoo call in spring. Her response wove together the delight and disgust that the cuckoo seems to elicit, announcing on social media: 'First cuckoo. Exciting until you remember what bastards they are.'[5]

Aristotle, the West's original natural historian, seems to have been mystified by the cuckoo. He devotes most of his entry on the cuckoo in *The History of Animals* to refuting ancient lore:

Common cuckoo (*Cuculus canorus*).

7

The cuckoo is said by some to be a hawk transformed, because at the time of the cuckoo's coming, the hawk, which it resembles, is never seen; and indeed it is only for a few days that you will see hawks about when the cuckoo's note sounds early in the season. The cuckoo appears only for a short time in summer, and in winter disappears.[6]

Aristotle goes on to point out similarities and differences between the cuckoo and the hawk, comparing their shape and plumage favourably while insistently contrasting the shape of their heads and talons. If his attempt to debunk the myth that the cuckoo becomes the hawk is less than convincing, it is because throughout his treatment of the cuckoo he just cannot let go of the hawk, even wrapping up by noting that the young of both the cuckoo and the hawk grow similarly 'fat and palatable'.

A few centuries later, following Aristotle closely, Pliny the Elder's *Natural History* grapples with the cuckoo's hawkish appearance to begin, and extols its tastiness to close: 'For sweetness of the flesh, there is not a bird in existence to be compared to the cuckoo at this season' – by which he meant soon after fledging. But while Aristotle tries, perhaps half-heartedly, to claim the cuckoo as a unique species, Pliny steps backward, grouping the cuckoo with the hawks and all but insisting that the cuckoo 'at a certain season of the year changes its shape . . . [and] its voice', however improbable such a transformation. Pliny notes that the cuckoo in its summer form lacks the hooked beak and talons of the hawk, but similarities between the birds' colouration and basic shape are too compelling to dismiss. Even so, he has to admit, cuckoos and hawks do sometimes cross paths, and when they do, the hawk will attack and even eat the cuckoo, making it 'the only one among the whole race of birds that is preyed upon by those of its own kind'. Pliny notes the common cuckoo's

tendency to parasitize smaller birds' nests, falsely (and grue-somely) claiming that when the young cuckoo is ready to leave the nest, it devours the 'foster-mother'.[7]

Aristotle and Pliny the Elder are right about just how similarly feathered the common cuckoo and the Eurasian sparrowhawk (*Accipiter nisus*) are. Both are counter-shaded, with darker backs and lighter undersides, and their chests and bellies are equally barred. Having evolved to mimic the sparrowhawk, the cuckoo benefits from being easily confused with a bird of prey, in that the presence of a cuckoo may scare potential hosts so that they abandon their nests long enough for the cuckoo to swoop in and lay her egg. At least, this works for the cuckoo sometimes. Some passerines likely to be preyed upon by hawks readily confuse their predators with cuckoos, while some likely to be parasitized by the

Sparrowhawk
(*Accipiter nisus*).

cuckoo can distinguish between hawks and cuckoos and react differently to them.[8]

The cuckoo family is not large, but its member species are quite diverse in size, plumage and behaviours. Their reproductive strategies have inspired many appearances in literature and other works of art as a metaphorical indicator that a character has an unfaithful spouse, or long-lost offspring, thanks to the fact that some cuckoos – including the familiar common cuckoo – are brood parasites. That is, these birds do not build their own nests or raise their own young. Instead, they deposit their eggs in the nests of other birds, leaving them to raise the cuckoo hatchling in competition with, or instead of, their own offspring: cuckoo hatchlings will readily nudge their hosts' eggs out of the nest. (You can see where Darwin, Yong and Roberts got the idea that cuckoos don't play nice.)

As a result, the common cuckoo has played a starring role in stories that link natural and human worlds. The cuckoo is not alone among animals in signifying absurdity or insanity (consider the comparable phrases 'crazy as a loon' or 'hare-brained'). More recently, the phrase 'cuckoo's egg' has done double duty as slang for computer-network hacking techniques in which cybercriminals deposit some type of malware in order to obtain a user's data or disrupt corporate or government system operations.[9] But fascination with the cuckoo's reproductive strategies yields some of its richest lore.

Etymologically speaking, the English word 'cuckoo' has onomatopoeic origins, deriving from the characteristic two-note song of the male during breeding season. 'Cuckold' derives from the word 'cuckoo' and is a generally unflattering term for a man with an unfaithful wife, however awkwardly the cuckoo's reproductive strategies map onto male ego and paternal anxiety – more on that later. This book will explore these bits and pieces of the stories we tell about the cuckoo – and with the cuckoo. After all, the common cuckoo is a great migrator, a beloved herald of spring in some of its habitats and the only animal after which a type of clock is named. As well, this chapter dips into the cuckoo's natural history.

The common cuckoo is a member of the order Cuculiformes, which contains only one family, Cuculidae, which also includes

Stamp printed in Tanzania, c. 1992.

the birds known as the coua, coucal, ani, koel, malkoha and roadrunner. Sometimes, a family that consists of a single species, the South American hoatzin (*Opthisthocomus hoazin*), is placed within the order Cuculiformes, but many sources dispute this claim. A recent major study published in 2005 lists 141 species in 32 genera; a 2012 volume adds three species and reorganizes some of the subfamilies in the largest group, Cuculinae, for a total of 144 species in 38 genera. Both sources agree to five major subfamilies.[10]

There seems to be little consensus regarding the accuracy of fossils identified as cuckoos in the Paleocene and Eocene, roughly 66–56 million years ago (MYA) and 55–34 MYA, respectively. While some studies have concluded that fossil tarsometatarsi (foot bones) or humeri (the first bone of the wing) should be recognized as belonging to the cuckoo family tree, Robert B. Payne, one of the foremost experts on avian behavioural ecology and evolution, finds certainty only in more recent descriptions, such as a fossil cuckoo, *Cursoricoccyx geraldinae* – an ancestor of the modern roadrunner – found in Colorado and dated to the early Miocene, about 20 MYA.[11] According to Payne, molecular genetic analysis indicates that the major cuckoo groups, and genetic distinctions between Old World and New World cuckoos, were already developing more than 60 MYA.[12]

Cuckoos are widely distributed and are found on every continent (but not in every habitat therein) except for Antarctica. Still, most cuckoo species spend the majority of their time in sub-Saharan Africa and throughout much of Asia. The breeding range of the common or European cuckoo stretches from the UK to Siberia, and from the northwest tip of Africa eastward through Japan. These birds spend their non-breeding months in Central and Southeast Africa, Sri Lanka and parts of the Indochinese Peninsula. Obviously, the bird sometimes called the European cuckoo is not as strictly European as it is colloquially known in some parts of the world.

One of the most consistent and striking characteristics of all members of the cuckoo family is zygodactyly. Most birds have three toes facing forward and one toe backward (anisodactyly, good for perching). In contrast, cuckoos have two toes forward, two toes back (good for climbing and walking). Although this characteristic is common to all cuckoos, it is not unique to cuckoos, as there are other bird families, including parrots and woodpeckers, that also boast zygodactyl feet. As well, cuckoos and their close kin have similar skeletal structure. The hypotarsus (a long bone that begins just below the joint corresponding to human ankles) sports two bony canals that are also found in

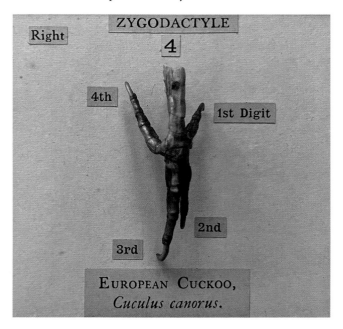

Common cuckoo's zygodactyl foot on display at the Museum of Natural History, London.

other zygodactyl birds, but their placement side-by-side is unique in the cuckoo family. Relative to body size, cuckoos tend to have long tails, and they moult annually. With some exceptions, members of the cuckoo family exhibit minimal sexual dimorphism: males and females are roughly the same size, shape and colour.

Otherwise, general descriptions of the cuckoo family indicate tremendous variation: 'The bill is usually slender and slightly arched. The plumage of most cuckoos is soft and lax. The body form varies among species with their systemic relationship, body size, and life style.'[13] The nostril can be oval or a thin slit; colouration varies among species; eyelashes can be absent, short or charmingly long.[14] While some long-extinct cuckoos may have been flightless, all current cuckoos can fly – but they exercise this skill in many different ways.[15] Long-distance migrators, flying thousands of kilometres twice annually, have long, pointed wings. Non-migratory members of *Cuculidae* have short, rounded wings. Accordingly, anis, couas, coucals and roadrunners are reluctant fliers, preferring to walk or run, though they may flutter to a perch. Arboreal cuckoos and those that practise brood parasitism tend to have smaller brains than their terrestrial and nesting relations. Ground-dwelling cuckoos have longer legs than those that spend most of their time in trees or in the air.

Like other birds, new members of cuckoo families are born in an undeveloped state, known as altriciality, and they require parental care. While most cuckoo babies have natal down, which is always more hair-like than fluffy, usually those belonging to brood-parasitic species are born naked, or at least lack down on their backs, making it easier for them to throw their weight against other eggs and nudge them out of the nest.[16] And while the plumage of most cuckoos is consistent in both juveniles and adults, some brood parasites have markedly distinct colouration at different life stages. The favourite foods of some types of adult cuckoo are hairy or spiny caterpillars, which are unpalatable to many other birds. Periodically, when caterpillar hairs and spines line its stomach, the lining of a cuckoo's stomach peels away. The cuckoo coughs it up, ridding itself of the nasty leftovers, and grows a new stomach lining.[17]

Greater roadrunner (*Geococcyx californianus*).

It is clear that the cuckoo family is diverse, in terms of reproductive and other behaviours, as well as in appearance. So what
distinguishes each subfamily within *Cuculidae*? The subfamily
Crotophaginae contains the New World cuckoos that live in groups,
often sharing nests. *Crotophaginae*'s mostly brown guira cuckoo
and three species of anis – the greater ani, smooth-billed ani
and groove-billed ani, all dressed in black feathers – occupy
overlapping territories stretching from southern Texas and Flor-
ida to all but the most southern and southwestern parts of
South America. Guiras are fine flyers, but anis are not; they tend
to nest low in trees. Many birds of all kinds have a uropygial (or
'preening') gland at the base of the tail and secrete an oil that
they use to care for their feathers. In the guira and the ani, this
gland is especially large, giving them a notoriously pungent
odour. Even though females of these species may lay their eggs

Smooth-billed ani
(*Crotophaga ani*).

Lesser ground cuckoo (*Morococcyx erythropygus*).

in a shared nest, in a form of cooperative breeding, there can still be competition among them, with eggs intentionally or accidentally being broken by adults of the species.

Neomorphinae contains five genera. Members of *Dromococcyx* (the pavonine and pheasant cuckoos) and *Tapera* (the striped cuckoo) are arboreal brood parasites found in Central and South America. Grouped together in *Neomorphus* are several elusive species of ground cuckoo that confine themselves to relatively small territories in the northern parts of South America. Among them, the banded ground cuckoo (*Neomorphus radiolosus*), occupying a sliver of the Chocó-Darién forest of Colombia and Ecuador, is considered endangered, owing to deforestation, by the International Union of Conservation of Nature (IUCN).[18] They have a range of calls and also click their beaks to communicate. The lesser ground cuckoo of Central America is the sole member of its genus, *Morococcyx*. It sports particularly striking eyes, which are ringed in yellow, with a splash of yellow in front and a lovely blue patch behind, framed with a black line reminiscent of kohl eyeliner. Only two species occupy *Geococcyx*: the greater and

Coucal (*Centropus sinensis*) chicks in their nest.

lesser roadrunners, *Geococcyx californianus* and *Geococcyx velox*, respectively. The greater roadrunner's range spans from the southwestern USA to Central Mexico; the lesser is found from Mexico to as far south as Nicaragua. They are poor flyers but fast runners, as their common name suggests. Unlike many members of the larger cuckoo family, male and female roadrunners form strong, monogamous pair bonds and share some parenting duties. Still, a greater roadrunner will lay an egg in another bird's nest once in a while, as if living out the old adage that warns, 'don't put all your eggs in one basket.'

All nine species of the coua making up the *Couinae* live in Madagascar. These nesting birds are among the most colourful of the larger cuckoo family, with plumage in greens, blues, pinks and purples. They also have startlingly bright blue featherless patches around their eyes. Mostly terrestrial, some hop or glide among the branches of trees, though none are strong long-distance fliers. The crested coua (*Coua cristata*) has a wonderful light grey mohican hairdo. While mouths of many birds include a colourful palate, the crested coua nestling's is bright red, with an unusual pair of white rings – unmistakable targets for parents doing the feeding.

The coucals constitute the genus *Centropus* and, within that genus, the subfamily *Centropodinae*. All coucals build their own unusually large nests from grasses. Also unusually (among cuckoos), males are slightly smaller than females and provide most parental care. Like most ground-dwelling birds, they have short, round wings; they also have, notably, a remarkably long claw on one of their back toes. More than two dozen species are spread across sub-Saharan Africa, the Arabian Peninsula, the Indian subcontinent, Southeast Asia, the Philippines, Indonesia and Australia.

Cuculinae is a large and diverse group. The malkohas are short-winged, long-tailed forest-dwellers who build their own nests and care for their own young.[19] They are among the most colourful

Crested coua
(*Coua cristata*).

African emerald cuckoo (*Chrysococcyx cupreus*).

cuckoos, and their feathers and beaks alike can vary greatly, a quality that is reflected in their common names: the blue-faced, green-billed, red-billed, chestnut-breasted, chestnut-bellied and black-bellied malkohas, to name a few. Like the couas, many types of malkohas have patches of colourful, featherless skin on their heads, usually around the eyes. Almost all are arboreal. Species of malkoha are found in Asia and Africa. Members of the genus *Coccyzus*, like malkohas, are long-tailed nesting birds, but they have long wings suitable for long-distance migrations. Most are based in South America, dividing their breeding and non-breeding time between the continent's more temperate south, where they breed, and the tropical north, where they pass the wintertime; basically, they jump the Tropic of Capricorn line. Some migrate between North and South America, while a few are year-round residents of Caribbean islands. One, the Cocos cuckoo (*Coccyzus ferrugineus*), lives only on Cocos Island, a Costa Rican national park some 550 kilometres (340 mi.) offshore in the Pacific Ocean.

Chestnut-breasted malkoha (*Phaenicophaeus curvirostris*) eating a common sun skink.

Perhaps the most storied member of *Cuculinae* is the brood parasite of the Old World, the bird known as the common cuckoo, *Cuculus canorus*, whose natural and cultural histories will occupy much of this book, with occasional visits to related members of the larger cuckoo family. During its breeding season, the common cuckoo can be found throughout Europe and Asia in all but the northernmost climes of Scandinavia and Russia, and southward to most of China and Central Asia, as well as in slivers of coastal Morocco and Algeria. Most common cuckoos winter in sub-Saharan Africa, avoiding the most arid southwestern part of the continent. It's a challenging migratory path, with survival depending on finding rest stops with food and water along the way. A smaller population retreats to winter homes in the Maldives, Sri Lanka and parts of Southeast Asia.

Even though common cuckoos are, well, common, they aren't so easy to spot. They are sometimes described as 'cryptic', meaning that their appearance, and their behaviours, allow them to blend

Cocos cuckoo
(*Coccyzus
ferrugineus*).

well into shadowy foliage. As adults, common cuckoos do tend to have a lot of dull grey plumage that sets off the sunflower-yellow iris and ring around the eye. The undersides of their wings, chests and tails are handsomely striped. While some types of birds are sensitive to ultraviolet light and therefore perceive colours differently to humans, common cuckoos probably see each other with the same neutral tones that we do. The melanin-based pigment in their feathers effectively absorbs light of all wavelengths, and their eyes lack the extreme uv vision more common among passerines.[20]

Eggs of the common cuckoo that are regularly found in the nests of various hosts, such as the goldcrest and sedge warbler.

It is often said that in its breeding grounds the common cuckoo is more readily heard than seen. William Shakespeare played on this elusiveness in *Henry iv, Part 1*, when the king recalls the downfall of his predecessor, Richard ii: 'He was but as the cuckoo is in June,/ Heard, but not regarded' (iii.2). Indeed, the male cuckoo makes his distinctive two-note call so frequently, and this simple song is so easily identifiable – and so identified with the arrival of spring – that clockmakers copied it for the iconic cuckoo-clock design that originated in the Black Forest in the eighteenth century. Female common cuckoos have their own song, which is often described as a chuckle.

At the American Museum of Natural History in New York, thirteen common-cuckoo eggs occupy a drawer in a tidily packed cabinet, one of many that contain the eggs of birds from all over the world. The cuckoo eggs are an ocean away from where they were laid, and they are now nested atop soft cream-and-pink-coloured padding in small cardboard boxes, alongside the eggs of their parasitized host. These eggs would have been collected and preserved by drilling a small hole through which the yolk and albumen would have been blown out. The cuckoo eggs are a little bit larger than the eggs they share a nest with, but they are still surprisingly small. The cuckoos would have quickly outsized their fellow nestlings if any of them had managed to survive the cuckoo's takeover of the nest. And they would have dwarfed their foster parents, even while depending on them for food. Female cuckoos tend to deposit their eggs in the nests of birds whose eggs will be similar to their own in colour and pattern. White-wagtail (*Motacilla alba*) eggshells are creamy, with brown dabs that look like they have been applied with a fine paintbrush and more dabs concentrated at the broader end of the egg. The cuckoo egg's base colour is a pale brown, but its own dabs of dark brown are remarkably similar to the marks on the wagtail eggs, as if drawn by the same hand.

The egg laid by a cuckoo in a reed bunting's nest, in contrast, has a lighter base than its host's eggs. Reed-bunting eggs are tawny with dark-brown splotches, more dribbled than dabbed. The cuckoo, in contrast, deposited a cream-coloured egg with mottled brown marks. Here the difference in size between host and guest egg is more pronounced. In the museum's collection, a cuckoo egg that is boxed with four greenfinch (*Chloris chloris*) eggs blends in extraordinarily well, being just a tad larger and almost indistinguishable in colour and pattern. Alongside two goldcrest (*Regulus regulus*) eggs, which are tiny – barely a centimetre lengthwise – the cuckoo egg is markedly larger, and shares with its hosts a relatively pointy tip.

How does the cuckoo manage to lay her eggs in a nest where the host eggs will be similar in colour and pattern to her own? Rather than picking and choosing each time she lays, or somehow adjusting the appearance of her eggs, the common cuckoo is instinctively habituated to parasitize one potential host for another, and she sticks closely to her first choice: a result of natural selection at work. If a cuckoo's egg closely resembles her host's eggs, she will have greater reproductive success. If her egg is very different, the chance that the host will recognize it as a foreign object and remove it from the nest increases. While the common cuckoo is recognized as one species, it splinters into groups according to which other bird it parasitizes: that is, one 'race' of common cuckoo always lays in reed-warbler nests, another in meadow-pipit nests and so on.[21]

Brood parasitism and egg mimicry are extraordinary behaviours. But so are many other behaviours of the common cuckoo (and its kin), including its arduous migration and its unique, instantly recognizable song. Extraordinary, too, are the many ways that humans have interpreted these behaviours, adapting them as fodder for our own stories of sexual fidelity, parental responsibility, mental instability and more. The chapters that follow explore what we know about this familiar bird, the common but elusive cuckoo, and the myths and metaphors that we have created around it.

2 'Dear Cuckold'

'It's quite a thing to ask, though, isn't it? . . .
quite a thing to ask of a man – when it isn't his baby?'
John Wyndham, *The Midwich Cuckoo* (1957)[1]

Some members of the cuckoo family engage in reproductive behaviours that have inspired humans' use of the bird in works of art. While most species of cuckoos do raise their own young, some, including the iconic common cuckoo, practise brood parasitism. In obligate brood-parasitic species, female cuckoos forego nesting. Instead, they lay their eggs in the nests of other birds, who, apparently unwittingly, incubate the eggs, which may mimic their own in colouration but are often larger. When they hatch, cuckoos are demanding babies, elbowing unhatched eggs or their smaller, weaker 'siblings' out of the nest, muscling to get more than their fair share of the food that their foster parents deliver.

In *On the Origin of Species*, Charles Darwin attributed the cuckoo's tendency 'to lay her eggs in other birds' nests' to sheer instinct, that great range of untaught, unlearned behaviours that are 'performed by an animal, more especially by a very young one, without experience and many individuals in the same way, without their knowing for what purpose [they are] performed'.[2] Why, then, don't all cuckoos lay their eggs in other birds' nests? Darwin notes that American cousins of the common European cuckoo tend to build their own nests, though they have at least occasionally been observed laying in the nests of blue jays and other birds (he likely means the yellow-billed and black-billed cuckoos, *Coccyzus americanus* and *Coccyzus erythropthalmus* respectively).

Utagawa Toyohiro, *Listening to the Cuckoo's Cry*, c. early 19th century, colour woodblock print.

John James
Audubon,
'Yellow-billed
Cuckoo', from
Birds of America
(1839–44).

He goes to great lengths to speculate how natural selection may
have established parasitism as a more frequent behaviour:

Now let us suppose that the ancient progenitor of our
European cuckoo had the habits of the American cuckoo,
and that she occasionally laid an egg in another bird's nest.
If the old bird profited by this occasional habit through
being enabled to migrate earlier or through any other
cause; or if the young were made more vigorous . . . then
the old birds or the fostered young would gain an advantage. And analogy would lead us to believe that the young
thus reared would be apt to follow by inheritance the
occasional and aberrant habit of their mother, and in their

turn would be apt to lay their eggs in other birds' nests, and thus be more successful in rearing their young. By a continued process of this nature, I believe it is that the strange instinct of our cuckoo has been generated.[3]

In other words, an 'aberrant' behaviour that results in greater reproductive success can become ingrained in generations of the animal's offspring.

But, as Darwin goes on to point out, avian parasitism isn't an act in which only the mother participates. It is completed by the offspring's self-interested actions. When the relatively large cuckoo hatches in the nest of another species, it usually forces unhatched eggs or fellow nestlings out, long before they fledge or can care for themselves. Alone in the nest, rather than sharing with its siblings, the cuckoo hatchling gets all the food

Black-billed cuckoo (*Coccyzus erythropthalmus*) and nest.

its unwitting foster parent or parents bring to the nest. While Darwin can't help but call this act a 'strange and odious instinct', he wonders if it might have arisen quite accidentally, through 'mere unintentional restlessness on the part of the young bird, when somewhat advanced in age and strength; the habit having been afterwards improved, and transmitted to an earlier age'.[4] It is as if the great naturalist couldn't quite attribute what looks like coolly calculated fratricide to the mere instincts of a baby bird. In the end, the gimlet-eyed scientist falls prey to Victorian sentiment.

Darwin was not the first to scold the cuckoo, nor would he be the last. In one of Aesop's fables, a 'lazy' cuckoo, 'too idle to make a comfortable home for herself and offspring', leaves her eggs for a hedge sparrow to incubate and raise.[5] Later the cuckoo complains to an owl that neither the hedge sparrow nor the recently fledged cuckoo chicks have shown gratitude for the cuckoo's wisdom in placing them so expertly together. Like a modern advice

Common cuckoo chick manipulating marsh warbler egg.

'The Cuckoo, the Hedge-Sparrow and the Owl', from Gallaher's Cigarette Card series *Fables and Their Morals*, 1922.

columnist, the owl turns tables on the cuckoo, suggesting that she apologize to both the hedge sparrow she has taken advantage of and the babies she has neglected. No doubt, this is a very human take on the matter, as surely no cuckoo ever looked back so bitterly after laying her egg. She would be way too busy preparing for her next egg, her next parasitic laying and, eventually, her long post-breeding migration.

Like it or not, cuckoos are not the only animals that practise brood parasitism. Brown-headed cowbirds (*Molothrus ater*) and their Central and South American relatives in the genus *Molothrus*, which live throughout North and Central America, do it too. So do members of the sub-Saharan bird family *Viduidae*, which includes indigobirds, whydahs and the aptly named cuckoo finches. Among insects, cuckoo bumblebees (genus *Bombus*) may be the only true brood parasites. Found in parts of North America, Europe, western Asia and North Africa, they lay their eggs in the nests of other bees. The cuckoo catfish (*Synodontis multipunctatus*) of Lake Tanganyika uses mouth-brooding cichlids as its host. While among cuckoo birds it is the female alone who locates and makes use of a host nest, the male and female cuckoo catfish

work together. After a female cichlid has laid her own eggs, and as she is scooping them into her mouth, the cuckoo catfish pair swoops in. The female deposits her eggs, the male fertilizes them and the cichlid unwittingly takes them in along with her own. The cuckoo-catfish eggs hatch first, just as baby cuckoo birds hatch before their hosts' own eggs, and the fish go a step further. They do not just elbow out the host's own eggs, but actually feed on them.

In the plant world, the cuckoo lends its name to *Cardamine pratensis*, which is known as the cuckoo flower or as 'lady's smock', an edible member of the brassica family (the cabbages and mustards) with pretty white or pink flowers. Native throughout Europe and western Asia, it is said to bloom as the first cuckoo arrives in spring.[6] Both *Arum maculatum* and *Arum italicum* have many common names. The former is also called 'jack in the pulpit' or 'cows and bulls', among other monikers; the latter is usually known simply as Italian arum. Both are sometimes called the cuckoo pint or cuckoo plant, names which bring together an archaic word for penis, 'pintle', and the relatively obscure use of 'cuckoo' (or 'cuckoo's nest') as a slang term for female genitals, a reference to the plant's spike-like yellow or purple spadix, which is nearly enveloped by a slender bract, a specialized leaf.[7]

In a less-than-straightforward linguistic move, the cuckoo's habit of laying her eggs in another bird's nest gave rise to the term 'cuckold'. Interestingly, while brood parasites take the greatest

Cuckoo pint (*Arum maculatum*): spathe and spadix with hairs and flowers, fruiting stem, leaf and tuber, watercolour zincograph after Mary Ann Burnett, c. 1853.

advantage of the parental labour of smaller nesting species that will raise the parasitic chick as their own, the term 'cuckold' and many of the metaphorical uses of cuckoos in literature are most often concerned with a lover's infidelity, but they are also used in tales of paternal anxiety, especially when a woman has given birth to a child whose biological father may not be her husband. Etymologically speaking, the English word 'cuckold' probably derives from the Old French equivalent *cucuault*, which in turn derives from the Old French word for cuckoo, *cocu*. 'Cuckold' became a zoomorphic insult used lavishly in literature; 'cuckquean', a term for a woman whose husband has committed adultery, is much more rarely used.[8]

Perhaps the first known usage in English is in a long comic poem of appropriately uncertain authorship, dating to the twelfth or thirteenth centuries: *The Owl and the Nightingale*. In this poem, two birds quarrel and sling insults at one another:

> Because of his abuse at home
> She'll seek out pleasures of her own;
> She'll cuckold him, of course she will,
> But don't say she's responsible.[9]

In this medieval work, the straying wife may be escaping from a cruel husband, but other literary cuckolders in the works that follow will not get off so easy. And not quite all writers portray cuckolded husbands as objects of derision.

Among the many literary scholars who haven't had much to say about cuckoos, but have pronounced upon cuckolds, Mark Millington and Alison S. Sinclair carefully distinguish the cuckold proper from the 'man of honour'. The former, they claim, is mocked for the situation he finds himself in – a situation that involves a husband whose wife has had a sexual relationship with

The Contented Cuckold.

Sould by John Owrton at the white horse neere the fountaine tauern without Newgate [corner
How bleff am I and what a happie life. in my conceite: hees more then mad, that
doe I inioy:well godamercie wife: (ffore to weare such pretious,profitable hornes
tis thou haft raisd my fortune all this Tobe a cuckold, why fhoold I repine?
thy occupation brings:and ten times more the difgrace is my wifes:the profit mine

Anonymous, after
François Langlois,
*The Contented
Cuckold* (1673),
engraving.

someone else. These characters are often the butt of jokes. Consider, for example, the elderly man January in Geoffrey Chaucer's
'Merchant's Tale' of the late fourteenth century. He actually wit-
nesses his wife's sexual encounter with a young groom but is so
gullible that she is able to convince him otherwise.[10] In contrast,
the latter type of cuckold, the 'man of honour', is 'admired for his

Juvenile common cuckoo with meadow pipit host.

attitude and action in the face of his wife's infidelity'.[11] What action could prompt admiration in such a situation? The authors cite characters in twentieth-century literature and stage plays who regain their honour by killing the faithless wife, her lover or both of them.[12] Wounded male egos re-establish themselves through acts of violence. Some honour! Millington and Sinclair take a Freudian turn into psychoanalytic theory, further informed by Melanie Klein, to describe this vengeful violence as emanating from an anxiety that structures patriarchy. The bearer of that anxiety tries to exert control over others, perceiving others (particularly women) as 'something that requires control'.[13] Exerting control, it would seem, takes place in the form of a display of power that asserts 'the *implied* sexual potency of the men who exercise that power'.[14] Claims of sexual potency and possession are at stake, because in 'cuckold' and 'man of honour' narratives alike, the man's wife has hooked up with someone else. This fact pokes and prods at his fragile ego until he displaces this threat to his own self-image by resorting to bloodshed.

By William Shakespeare's time, three centuries after Chaucer, the literary trope of cuckoldry was very well established. It appears throughout Shakespeare's *oeuvre*, in both the tragedies and the comedies. One Shakespeare scholar goes so far as to claim that the playwright created nothing less than a 'community of cuckolds'.[15] But as Cristina León Alfar points out, writers in the English Renaissance, including Shakespeare and others, were less interested in having their female characters commit adultery than they were in devising male fantasies, 'stories that are not true', of wifely betrayal, shaped by masculine narcissism, jealousy and paranoia.[16] In an era in which they lacked basic rights to divorce or own property, women had little power to protest their husbands' unfaithfulness. But a man's failure to maintain order at home

Isaac Cruikshank, *The Cuckold Departs for the Hunt*, c. 1800, pen and ink with watercolour on paper.

– which encompassed the behaviours of his wife – could shatter his reputation and shake the foundation of his power in other realms, even if the offending acts were largely fabricated for dramatic effect.

This type of unfounded jealousy is a familiar ingredient in Shakespearean stews of rumour-mongering, masquerade and mistaken identities. Examples abound, but a few will suffice.[17] In *The Merry Wives of Windsor*, Ford's wife is one of two married women who are being pursued by Falstaff – women, by the way, who are determined not only to fend off Falstaff's advances but to humiliate him. Ford believes that his wife is taking the flirtation seriously and decries his possible cuckolding as just about the worst thing he can imagine: '"Cuckold", "Wittoll", "Cuckold"!/ The devil himself hath not such a name' (II.2).

In *Cymbeline*, Posthumus, exiled far away from his lover Imogen, gets mixed up in a wager with Iachimo, who claims that Imogen is not as faithful as Posthumus would like to think. When Iachimo boasts that he has successfully seduced her – a lie – Posthumus adopts the stance of the 'man of honour' and issues a threat: 'If you will swear you have not done't, you lie,/ And I will kill thee if thou dost deny/ Thou'st made me cuckold' (II.4).

In *Othello*, the title character goes even further, leaping from suspicion to violence. Goaded by Iago to fear that his wife, Desdemona, is cheating on him, Othello declares, 'I will chop her into messes! Cuckold me?' (IV.1) and later proves it was no idle threat by smothering her to death.

Embedded in the epithet 'cuckold', when it is found in Shakespeare's plays, is its root, the cuckoo itself, the bird that refuses to pair-bond and expects other birds to rear its young. Cuckoos dart in and out of Shakespeare's plays, too, alongside the many cuckolds, announcing the arrival of spring as often as they suggest infidelity. But the cuckoo is not the only animal to haunt the man whose wife strays, or is suspected (often unfairly) of straying. In the sixteenth and seventeenth centuries, 'horn jokes' were a popular means of disparaging a man's masculinity and smearing his wife's reputation at the same time, as if it were terribly funny to call a man a cuckold behind his back – or to his face. Even worse, the Middle English insult *witewold* (now spelled as 'wittol') describes the man who knows that his wife has at least one other lover and tolerates his own disgrace, in a sort of portmanteau of the verb *witen* (meaning 'to know') and a shortened form of 'cuckold'. So-called horn humour could be not only verbal but visual, in caricatures, or in the public humiliation of seeing horns nailed to one's front door. It may seem odd that the cuckold grows the weapon-like horns of a bull or buck. These animals may appear to be regal or powerful, but they are also potential prey – just as the cuckold is prey to his wife's deception and the derision of his peers. Some see the horn motif as 'a kind of displacement, in which the horniness of the cuckolder ends up manifesting itself on the brow of the insufficiently masculine cuckoldee', that is, showing up as a symptom of his loss of status.[18]

Writers using the cuckoo metaphor in tales of infidelity or parenting mix-ups often stretch, twist and turn it until the literary figure of the cuckoo bears little resemblance to its real-world referent. For example, in the novel *Cuckoo's Egg* by science-fiction writer C. J. Cherryh, the apparent 'cuckoo's egg' is an infant human, the only one on the planet. The boy, named Thorn, is raised under the care of a male character named Duun, a great warrior of the hatani. Duun is a Shonun, a member of a humanoid yet thoroughly furred species, with clawed hands and pointed ears that move expressively, a characteristic that earthly primates have largely lost. Duun teaches Thorn, often violently, the ways of the hatani, and allows him to be subjected to medical examination and experimentation. True to form, Duun may be a *sort* of cuckold,

Detail of Samuel Scott, *A Morning, with a View of Cuckold's Point*, c. 1750–60, oil on canvas. Note the horns atop a post, indicating the presence of a cuckold.

in that he invests parental care into a child that he did not himself father. But if Thorn is not Duun's biological son, whose is he? No one's, really. Thorn, it turns out, was engineered in a laboratory from genetic material scavenged from the last living human aboard a spaceship against which Duun had led a fierce two-year battle.[19] No reed warbler or meadow pipit ever went to so much trouble to bring a voracious baby cuckoo into their nest.

The Midwich Cuckoos (1957) by John Wyndham, one of several pen names of the prolific science-fiction writer, wields the cuckoo metaphor more persuasively. In this novel, all the residents of a fictional English village (including the animals) collapse, only to wake up several hours later with no recollection of what has happened. The women in the village soon realize they are all pregnant – married, single and postmenopausal alike; some were sexually active before this odd event, others not yet or no longer. For some, this is cause for alarm, for others, celebration, at least until they realize that there is something very strange about the pregnancies. The children are born on an accelerated schedule, just as a cuckoo egg tends to hatch before the host species' own eggs. And they mature rapidly into eerily similar golden-eyed, flax-haired, glaring prodigies. Much like the distinctively marked, outsized cuckoo hatchlings who announce their incessant hunger to their adoptive parents, the Midwich children are demanding bullies. In a twist likely inspired by ants or bees rather than the birds, the children

Reed warbler feeding juvenile common cuckoo.

seem to share a hive mind. When one learns a new skill, the others obtain it as well, even if they are not present to observe. They begin to frighten the villagers, and tension escalates to violence.

Here, the cuckoo metaphor is an apt enough fit, with one awkward turn: the women of Midwich play the role of a host species' nest – given that these alien children were somehow implanted in their uteruses – rather than the role of the clever female cuckoo, who drops off her eggs and goes on her merry way while palming off the labour of parental care to unwitting foster parents. The screenplay for the taut 1960 adaptation *Village of the Damned*, directed by Wolf Rilla, avoids explicitly mentioning the cuckoo. Additional remakes would follow, in John Carpenter's *Village of the Damned* (1995) and a British TV series, *The Midwich Cuckoos*, which aired in 2022. But the source novel lets the metaphor fly. Most of the mentions of cuckoos are preoccupied with the feelings of the mysteriously cuckolded men of the village. Occasionally, an adult character is able to imagine the children's point of view: 'I'm simply doing my best to place myself in the situation of a young cuckoo. As such, I fancy I should resent anything that appeared likely to lessen attention to my comfort and well-being.'[20] Here the cuckoo looms large as a greedy creature, however immature, all the while overtaxing the wishful breeding pair responsible for its upbringing.

As the tension escalates dangerously in Midwich, the men of the village become rattled and worried, while the women generally go about their maternal duties as if everything were perfectly fine: 'They all *know* well enough now that, biologically speaking, they are not even their own children, but they did have the trouble and pain of bearing them – and that . . . isn't the kind of link they can just snip and forget.'[21] Among the birds, it is not only the female of the host species that feeds the cuckoo nestling. The male partner of the warbler, pipit or other host joins in the care of the voracious interloper. Meanwhile, in Midwich, the men gather at the pub, distancing themselves from the children who now occupy their households, suspecting their wives of infidelity and plotting their revenge.

The horror film *Vivarium* (2019), directed by Lorcan Finnegan, puts the cuckoo in its very first scenes, in close-ups of a cuckoo hatchling forcing, first, an egg, and then, a smaller hatching out of its host's nest. As a juvenile, not yet fledged, the cuckoo shrieks and looms over its foster parent who comes to feed it. When a schoolchild finds the naked baby birds dead on the ground, her teacher Gemma (played by Imogen Poots), calmly explains, 'that's nature, that's just the way things are,' but one can imagine that her rational response to the sight might have changed by the end of the film. She and her boyfriend (Jesse Eisenberg) find themselves trapped in a bizarre housing development by a mysterious estate agent; as if they didn't already feel confused and confined, suddenly, an infant appears. The boy proves to be mocking, screeching, voracious, fast-growing and inscrutable – an unwanted child foisted onto surrogate parents who, however unwilling, are unable to resist his demands. Although the bird itself never re-appears after the early synecdochical scenes, *Vivarium* spins brood parasitism into a kind of trauma likely not shared by the meadow pipit or dunnock or warbler.

Some of the best-known and most indulgent uses of the cuckoo/ cuckold label are associated with the Irish writer James Joyce and his partner Nora Barnacle. They met in 1904, married in 1931 and were seldom separated until Joyce's death in 1941. In 1912 Joyce seems to have stood by happily while Barnacle entertained the flirtations of another man, a close family friend. He even egged her on (pardon the near pun) for a while. Eventually, fearing that the game had gone too far, Joyce confronted the man and banished him from their inner circle, which was hardly surprising, given

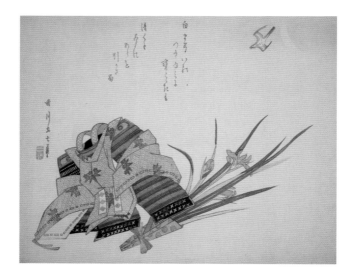

Harukawa Goshichi, *Crescent Moon with Flying Little Cuckoo*, 1825, colour woodblock print.

his obsessive attachment to Barnacle.[22] His tendency to become jealous at any provocation – and for both Joyce and Barnacle to bait that jealousy – was so ingrained in their relationship that in 1917, during a brief solo holiday, Barnacle began a letter to Joyce, notoriously, with the words 'Dear Cuckold'.[23]

Maybe Joyce was titillated by the thought of his spouse having sex with someone else, aroused by his own jealousy. Maybe he revelled in Nora's taunts, in which case she might have even more cleverly addressed him as 'Dear Wittol'. Sexual frankness was part and parcel of their relationship. During a brief separation in 1909, they exchanged letters that later became renowned for their unfettered sexual explicitness and erotic scatology. It is assumed that Nora's letters were also ribald; only Joyce's letters survive. Some speculate that Joyce engineered opportunities to ignite jealousy, create conflict or unleash curious fantasies in order to develop material that would later appear in his books.

Leopold Bloom, a protagonist of Joyce's *Ulysses* (1922), may be the best-known literary figure haunted by the cuckoo. His wife, Molly Bloom, who shares more than a few characteristics with Nora Barnacle, is having an affair with the singer Hugh 'Blazes' Boylan, an affair that Leopold is all too aware of. She lusts briefly after Stephen Dedalus, a friend of her husband's.[24] Bloom himself seems ever on the verge of being exposed, humiliated or punished. A character identified as 'The Crier' announces to anyone who cares to listen that 'Leopold Bloom of no fixed abode is a well-known dynamitard, forger, bigamist, bawd and cuckold and a public nuisance to the citizens of Dublin.'[25] Here and there in *Ulysses*, a cuckoo-clock calls the time, as if to startle characters out of their reveries, erotic and otherwise.[26] Mere mention of the bird, or the clock that mimics its call, is a mocking taunt, here in a line Joyce cribbed from Shakespeare's own *Love's Labour's Lost*: 'Cuckoo! Cuckoo! Cuck [Buck] Mulligan clicked lewdly. O word of fear!'[27]

Like modernist literature, modern pornography has its own cuckoo, a genre mainly involving men who enjoy watching their female partners have sex with other men. From porn, the term

Bowl with cuckoo and moon design in raised relief, Hirado Mikawachi ware, Japan, first half of 20th century.

47

Honoré-Victorin Daumier, 'There goes my wife!! Oh, the wretch, while I'm having a shave she's making a cuckold of me!', plate 22 from *Moeurs Conjugales* (1840).

'cuckold' migrated to 'alt-right' digital platforms, was shortened to 'cuck' and is now wielded as a slur. This is, after all, a milieu shaped by white nationalism and dubious aggrievement, and prone to vitriol and violence that targets women, LGBTQ+ communities, Jews and people of colour. In this discourse, the portmanteau 'cuckservative' is a sneering label slapped by extremists onto those they perceive as insufficiently masculine or holding political views not shared by the far right.[28] But an insult with such a rich history cannot be confined to back channels and extremist message boards. In July 2023 one of the world's wealthiest men threw the slur publicly at another of the world's wealthiest men. 'Zuck is a cuck,' tweeted Elon Musk, owner of Tesla, SpaceX and Twitter (now X), taunting his rival Mark Zuckerberg, whose company Meta had just added a Twitter-like platform called Threads to its stable of social media products.[29] The vulgar quips of tech bros amplified by digital megaphones were a long way from avian-inspired Shakespearean plot device, Joycean tease or sci-fi thought experiment – or were they?

THE CUCKOO

Sir Archibald Geikie, extract from *Birds of Shakespeare* (1916).

But let us return to the birds. No matter what we think of the cuckoo's reproductive routines, our thoughts are of little concern to them. Unsettled by their willingness to mate with multiple partners in a season – or titillated? They'll do it anyway. Appalled by the female cuckoo laying her eggs in other birds' nests? She's probably been doing it longer than *Homo sapiens* has walked the

Earth. Shocked that a cuckoo hatchling has the wherewithal to get rid of its nestmates? Instead, one might wonder at the wild diversity of behaviours in the natural world.

Stephen Dedalus of *Ulysses* gets the last word on the subject. Very far from the actual end of Joyce's famously languorous novel, Dedalus addresses the subject of cuckoldry amid delirious debate regarding Shakespeare's protagonists (weaving in a reference to Georges Bizet's opera *Carmen*, 1875): 'The boy of act one is the mature man of act five. All in all. In *Cymbeline*, in *Othello*, he is bawd and cuckold. He acts and is acted upon. Lover of an idea or a perversion, like José he kills the real Carmen.'[30] Dedalus makes way for the cuckold to become the 'man of honour', rather than a comic dupe. Even more interestingly, he situates cuckoldry as just another life experience, perhaps a rite of passage, an inevitability, a piece of a totality, an expected variation in human sexual relations. In that light, can the cuckold be viewed without judgement? Maybe not in this lifetime. After all, Dedalus goes on to name-check Hamlet in a reverie describing a heaven where 'there are no more marriages, glorified man, an androgynous angel, being a wife unto himself'.[31] In this fantasy, the wife suspected of breaking her marital vows is not only blamed or punished but erased. Dedalus puts us – at least for a time – in a forest in which the calling cuckoo, always male, can sing his song without being bothered by a response. And the female, with her 'strange and odious' habits and her 'murderous' offspring, is nowhere to be found. As is so often the case, allegories and analogies, fables and fantasies populated by animals say much more about human fears and desires than about animal life – however cuckoo this may seem.

3 Myth and Madness

'There was no immunity to cuckoo ideas on Earth.'
Kurt Vonnegut, *Mother Night* (1962)

A well-travelled bird, the common cuckoo appears in our myths and metaphors, our folk tales and popular culture. Many of these usages involve sexual relationships, playing on the cuckoo's curious habit of laying her eggs in another bird's nest in stories of adultery or uncertain parentage, a frequent Shakespearean trope. Others evoke the cuckoo's steadfastness, drawing on the predictability of its migrations and its status as a sign of spring's arrival: the cuckoo plays a part in the Hindu festival Holi, which celebrates Kamadeva, the god of love, desire and eroticism, whose actions ensure fertility and reproductive success. At a totally different affective register, the bird's name can be invoked as an accusation that one is just plain crazy. Despite the cuckoo's rich ancient history, the humorist P. G. Wodehouse usually gets credit for bringing the cuckoo into twentieth-century slang. In one of his short stories, he dashes off the line 'the boy seemed cuckoo' when the young man in question, 'Bingo' Little, hems and haws, stalling clumsily when he must announce to a friend that he is now married.[1]

There are any number of explanations for why 'cuckoo' so readily became a synonym for varying degrees of silliness or mental illness. One arises from the seemingly foolish behaviour of laying an egg in another bird's nest. The call of the male, from which the cuckoo derives its onomatopoeic name, might also

Common cuckoo in flight.

53

Zheng Fu, *Poetic Maxim*, 1691, hanging scroll, ink on paper. Translation: 'He who acts like the single-minded cuckoo will not make mistakes. If a gentleman upholds this code of conduct, he will enjoy a happy and long life.'

inspire a human to disparage the bird, since at certain times of year the two-note song seems to be sung relentlessly, as a person might blather maniacally without respite. The repetitiveness of the cuckoo's call has long been recognized – at times with some irritation – by those who hear it. In one of Aesop's sixth-century BCE fables, a bee quarrels with a cuckoo, calling his tune 'a tiresome unvaried song'. When the cuckoo accuses the bee of being similarly redundant in building hive after identical hive, the bee wins the argument by defending its own 'labours' as useful, and reminding the cuckoo that in 'works of taste and amusement, monotony is of all things to be avoided'.[2] Of course, we will never know if the cuckoo aspired to artistry, or if he believes his song – a territorial announcement and a mating call, no less – to be utilitarian.

The cuckoo also surfaces in the vast menagerie of creatures that serve as avatars and companions to the gods of ancient Greece, especially those of the Greek goddess Hera and her counterpart in Roman mythology, Juno. Hera, the goddess of women, marriage and childbirth, was associated with cattle, the peacock and, importantly, the cuckoo. Zeus – her own brother, known as Jupiter to the Romans – transformed himself into a cuckoo to seduce her: 'Didst not thou, Zeus, become a wandering bird,/ To win the love of one who drove a herd?'[3]

After all, that was Zeus' schtick, turning himself into an animal, or occasionally a flame, to insinuate himself with the objects of his desire. As a spectacular white bull, he charmed Europa and swam with her on his back to Crete, where he raped her. Zeus raped Leda while in the form of a swan. As a result, Leda may have laid an egg or two, from which hatched her children: Helen and Pollux, fathered by Zeus, and Clytemnestra and Castor, fathered by Leda's husband, Tyndareus, king of Sparta. Accounts of the relationship between Zeus and Hera vary, but popular versions suggest that Zeus, being the god of the sky, created a terrible storm that caused Hera to seek shelter as she climbed Mount Thornax. As she rested, Zeus, in the shape of a cuckoo, flew to her lap and shivered pitiably. As she comforted the animal, he retook his humanoid form and made his move. She may have resisted for any number of reasons. Zeus was her brother, her rapist and a deceiver, to boot. And yet, Hera, the goddess of marriage herself, went on to marry Zeus. Throughout their marriage, she raged jealously against his other lovers and pitched battles

A. Rey and Kaeppelin, *Juno and the Cuckoo*, 1844–61, lithograph.

with the children he fathered with them: recall her constant torment of Heracles. Among the many symbols that accompany representations of Hera in statuary and pottery, one might find a cuckoo. Whether it is a reminder of the goddess's fondest memories of a favoured bird or of her tempestuous liaison is for only her to know.

Hera's divine duties did not extend specifically to motherhood, but in other traditions the cuckoo bears moral messages, involving maternal ideals. The Exeter Book, a late tenth-century manuscript, contains a treasure trove of Old English poetry and a set of approximately ninety riddles. One of them, Riddle 9, describes the young cuckoo's abandonment by its biological

Juno and Her Cuckoo, 2nd–3rd century, terracotta oil lamp.

parents, in melodramatically anthropomorphized language: 'I was endowed with life amongst those unrelated to me. The protective lady [the host nesting bird] then fed me until I grew up and could set out on wider journeys. She had fewer dear sons and daughters because she did so.'[4] This might sound like an odd sort of mothering to admire – one that is so devoted to the offspring of another than she sacrifices her own – but the English scholar Jennifer Neville points out that it was common in the era for children to be relinquished, or taken in, for economic reasons, among others. For example, nursemaids raised royal children, likely at the expense of their own, and one could rest assured this was a noble act.[5] Alternatively, she suggests, the cuckoo in the riddle might be a 'sinful thought' that, when nurtured, drives out the good and holy.[6]

In China, too, cuckoo symbolism is multivalent. In Confucian writing and other texts, the common cuckoo is called *shijiu* (alternatively spelled *jie ju*) or *bugu*, names imitative of its characteristic call, and associated with the arrival of spring and a prompt to plant crops.[7] Nothing unusual there. Elsewhere in Old Chinese lore, *dujuan* is the cuckoo who calls incessantly, the 'plaintive bird' associated with an emperor who 'with Zeus-like prowess . . . seduced his prime minister's wife, but was later forced to abdicate', his soul living on as a cuckoo after his fall from power.[8] But in an interesting precedent to the Exeter riddle involving the cuckoo's assignment of parental duties to other birds, at least one strand of Chinese lore upholds brood parasitism as a sign of 'nobility, for nest-building and care of the cuckoo's offspring by other birds are viewed as deferring to the status and virtue of the cuckoo – analogous to the homage paid to an exemplary ruler'.[9] Rather than being an exploiting, nasty interloper, the cuckoo chick must be special enough to demand slavish attention from its host.

In a collection of Bhutanese folk tales, the cuckoo plays a role in another complex domestic drama, this one involving an inter-species romance. In the tale, a male cuckoo and a female pigeon marry and, forming a family, successfully hatch two chicks. As the seasons change, the cuckoo does what all common cuckoos must do, which is migrate south. As he takes flight, he promises his pigeon-wife that he will be back in the spring. A hawk, seeing the cuckoo depart and recognizing that the pigeon now has sole responsibility for the nestlings, starts hanging around, planting the idea that the cuckoo will never return and coaxing her to take him as her new husband. In her loneliness, in the cold of winter, the pigeon accepts the hawk's advances. When she leaves the nest to look for food, he takes first one, then the other chick away, and kills and eats them both. Lying to the distraught pigeon, the hawk blames the cuckoo for their disappearance. Eventually, he kills and eats her too.

The cuckoo does return in spring, as he had promised. Why would he do otherwise? But of course, the nest is empty, and his family is nowhere to be found. The duplicitous hawk gets the last word: 'Your wife grieved to death and the children went in search of you.'[10] The lesson seems to be threefold. First, that a wife who does not fully trust her husband will dig her own grave. Second, that a man with a peripatetic personality might find that after a

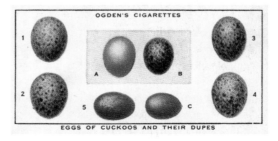

Eggs of cuckoos and their dupes, from the Ogden's Cigarettes *Colour in Nature* series.

too-long absence he will have no home to return to. And finally, that each will act according to their nature. The pigeon seeks to flock and abhors being alone. The hawk is a carnivore and sees just about any smaller creature, even another bird, as a potential meal, so long as it is not of its own type. And finally, the common cuckoo must migrate – and just as surely will return.

While many cuckoo myths and metaphors involve uncertain parentage and extra-marital affairs, in India the Chataka bird – the Jacobin cuckoo, *Clamator jacobinus* – is a symbol of the purest love. It is said to drink only the purest raindrops that fall from the sky, and to avoid the Earth's abundant-but-polluted bodies of water. Prominently crested, the bird appears to have a second beak that points constantly skyward, which is regarded as another sign of its unflappable allegiance to Rama, one of the incarnations of the deity Vishnu.[11]

Japanese folklore and artworks employ a cuckoo – *hototogisu* (*Cuculus poliocephalus*, the lesser cuckoo) – for multiple purposes. A folktale such as 'The Cuckoo Brothers' proffers an

Lesser cuckoo (*Cuculus poliocephalus*).

explanation for the cuckoo's persistent call. In one version of the story, the younger brother feeds his elder brother, who is blind. The elder becomes suspicious that his brother is saving the best food for himself. Tearing at his brother's throat, he finds only shells and roots. With the younger brother now dead, the gods instruct the elder to call 1,008 times each day to ask for forgiveness.[12] In a haiku by the seventeenth-century poet Bashō, the lesser cuckoo is recognized for its attractive call and its association with summertime, rather than spring, and the summer's maturing grain crops:

Hototogisu (Cuckoo)
Maneku ka mugi no (Were you invited by the barley)
Mura Obana (Plumed with seed?)[13]

In nineteenth-century woodblock prints by Japanese artists, the cuckoo is often depicted in a dynamic diagonal side view, as if falling or diving towards land, the downward motion suggesting tragedy, mourning or oncoming storms. Especially if depicted in visual art or literature passing over mountains, the cuckoo is a messenger capable of passing between the earthly world and the afterlife.[14]

In European folklore, the cuckoo sometimes plays the role of a kind of fortune-teller. James Hardy, a storied Victorian-era naturalist, catalogued dozens of ditties, aphorisms, poems and other references to the cuckoo, finding the bird most frequently linked to seasonal cycles. In a popular rhyme that had many regional variations:

> The cuckoo comes in April,
> Sings a song in May,
> Then in June another tune,
> And then he flies away.[15]

Hardy found that some versions of the rhyme speak directly to how the cuckoo's migration criss-crosses with crop cycles:

> The cuckoo comes in the middle of March,
> And sings in the middle of April;
> And passes away at the Lammas-tide,
> When the corn begins to fill.[16]

The cuckoo is a seasonal harbinger here of the arrival of not only spring but spring's midpoint or thereabouts, when Lammas Day is invoked. This 'Loaf Mass' or 'First Fruits' holiday takes place on 1 August or shortly thereafter, when the cuckoo should be long gone. It is also a token of luck, good and bad. In Germany, the

Ando Hiroshige, *Cuckoo*, c. 1840s, colour woodblock print.

Dionisio Minaggio, cuckoo from *Il bestiario barocco* (The Feather Book, 1618), a handmade book composed mostly of feathers, by the Chief Gardener of the State of Milan.

cuckoo might be a sign of good weather, but in Switzerland, if a cuckoo comes close to town, it's considered an omen that foul weather might be on its way. In both countries, hearing the cuckoo after 24 June, St John's Day, indicates that the grape harvest and the quality of wine will be poor.[17] Some European farmers might have long timed their planting to the first call of the cuckoo, but in parts of Scandinavia the number of times the cuckoo calls predicts how long until one marries, or dies, and whether it is

CVCHA

heard from north or south, to the right or left, predicts prosperity or despair, a life long or short.[18] In France, hearing a cuckoo call when you have money in your pocket, and giving those coins a shake, assures you of financial security. When in Bulgaria, you will want to have a full belly as well as money in your pocket when you hear the cuckoo, so as to bring forth good luck; in Ukraine, hearing a cuckoo call when you are hungry or your purse is empty is a bad omen.[19]

In Germany, the rituals that must be undertaken when hearing the first cuckoo get more complicated, and the results more targeted:

> A German peasant does the same thing as when he hears thunder for the first time for that year; he rolls himself several times on the grass, and is thereby insured against pains of the back for that season, and all the more effectually if the bird continues to call while he is on the ground.[20]

But perhaps nowhere does one need to take more specific immediate measures when hearing the season's first cuckoo than in parts of Scotland, where the cuckoo may be called the 'gowk'. There, when the cuckoo calls, remove your shoes and socks and check the soles of your feet for an errant hair. (There is some quarrel about whether the right foot or the left is a more reliable sage.) You will someday marry someone with hair the same colour as the one stuck to your foot. There are nearly endless variations of these superstitions anywhere that the common cuckoo lands. So, just to be on the safe side, the next time cuckoos are due to arrive wherever you might be, don't get within earshot if your stomach is growling, and once you hear the bird call, jingle any loose change in your pocket, roll on the ground and inspect your bare feet. You might just get lucky. But be careful when in Scotland on Gowk

Day (also known as Hunt the Gowk or Huntigowk Day); the joke might be on you, since it's April Fool's Day to the rest of us.[21] You might end up being the gowk – the butt of the joke – yourself.

While in these many myths and bits of folklore the cuckoo sets a fine example, imports essential information or brings good fortune (or bad), the idea that the cuckoo is not quite sane was also established long ago. The playwright Aristophanes made this clear in his comic play *The Birds*, which is believed to have been first performed in 414 BCE. Aristophanes dubbed a fantastical city in the sky *Nephelococcygia*, translated as 'Cloud Cuckoo Land'. Euelpides and Pisthetaerus, the two human protagonists, implore the hoopoe Epops, king of the birds, to consider building a city in the sky. Epops calls together all the birds to confer. The cuckoo is one of many who heed the call, and the gathering mob is initially – and understandably – appalled at the idea of men living among them. But the plan for the city in the sky proves irresistible. The birds once knew power (or so Pisthetaerus says), with each species lording over another city or region. It was the cuckoo who ruled

Cast of *The Birds of Aristophanes* at the Theatre Royal, Cambridge, November 1883.

Egypt and Phoenicia, ordering his subjects to harvest grain with the call 'Cuckoo! cuckoo! go to the fields, ye circumcised.'[22] Given the chance, the birds could not resist seeking power again, building their city in the sky to block earthly tributes from reaching the gods, and controlling all traffic between these realms. Why shouldn't the birds assert themselves? Humanity hardly appreciates all the work they do to control pests and herald the changing of the seasons, but rather treats the once 'great and sacred' birds as things to be trapped, sold and roasted.[23]

The name of the city does not honour the cuckoo, who plays a relatively minor role in the play. Instead, 'Cloud Cuckoo Land' calls out the lunacy of the scheme hatched by two disaffected Athenians and a multispecies bevy of birds. To build a city between heaven and earth sounds as silly as dropping one's egg in another bird's nest, doesn't it? In the end, however, both schemes prove strategic triumphs, diverting resources in support of the schemers' own self-interests.

The habit of calling on the cuckoo as a sign of lunacy (to mix one's metaphors a bit) persisted, even blossomed, through the early twentieth century, and not only in Wodehouse's adoption of the term in his stories about the manservant Jeeves. In 1924 the journalist and critic Gilbert Seldes, writing under the pseudonym Vivian Shaw, used the pages of *Vanity Fair* to label the kind of pun-mad, downright Dadaist comedy then dominating the vaudeville scene as the 'cuckoo school of humour'.[24] Not that any birds were involved, rather that the style seemed like the verbal analogue to the physical comedy of slapstick cinema. Rosalind Sayre Smith, sister and sister-in-law, respectively, to Zelda and F. Scott Fitzgerald, once referred to the couple's boozy years in New York City around 1920 as their 'cuckoo days'.[25]

More ominous mentions of the cuckoo appear in Ken Kesey's 1962 novel *One Flew Over the Cuckoo's Nest*, which is set in a chaotic

Utagawa Hiroshige and Uoya Eikichi, *Azuma Bridge from Komagatado Temple*, 1857, woodblock print with ink and colour on paper.

psychiatric institution. The narrator, Chief Bromden, describes the mutterings of a fellow patient, evoking the same ceaseless repetitiveness that Aesop's bee found in the cuckoo's song, but with much greater mournfulness, even desperation: 'It's like an old clock that won't tell time but won't stop neither, with the hands bent out of shape and the face bare of numbers and the alarm bell rusted silent, an old worthless clock that just keeps ticking and cuckooing without meaning nothing.'[26] The incessant call of the clock isn't the only cuckoo in the novel. Late in the book, when both Chief Bromden and his friend Randle McMurphy are forced to undergo a brutal form of electroshock therapy, the chief begins a delirious monologue stewing together sensations experienced during the treatment, memories

Playbill designed by Sharon W. Houk for a production of *One Flew Over the Cuckoo's Nest* performed by the Phoenix Stage Company in Oakville, Connecticut, 14–28 July 2018.

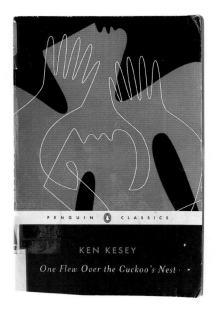

Cover designs for Ken Kesey, *One Flew Over the Cuckoo's Nest* (1962) and John Nichols, *The Sterile Cuckoo* (1965).

of his upbringing and his grandmother's funeral, a torrent of hallucinations and fragments of a nursery rhyme: 'Three geese inna flock . . . one flew east, one flew west, one flew over the cuckoo's nest . . . o-u-t spells out . . . goose swoops down and plucks you out'.[27]

Most explorations of Kesey's novel find in these lines that the 'cuckoo's nest' – the phrase itself a non sequitur in relation to an obligate brood parasite – serves as a metaphor for the psychiatric unit, which, in contrast to the purposeful geese heading east or west, is a site of directionless chaos and coercion and fantasies of escape that eventually become tragically true. The goose, it would seem, is McMurphy, whose antics provoke the nurse in charge, Miss Ratched, and empower patients to defy her authority. In the end, too, his demise opens the door for the chief's escape: just as in the rhyme – and the children's game played while singing along – a goose 'plucks' one lucky soul out of the nest.[28]

Another portrait of mental illness published in the 1960s is John Nichols's novel *The Sterile Cuckoo* (1965), in which a love affair between two university students devolves into drunken malaise. Near the end of the novel, the whimsical, garrulous, impulsive Pookie Adams writes a poem to her conflicted lover, Jerry Payne, as she teeters between recognizing that their relationship is ending – and her grip on reality is giving way to suicidal ideation – and begging him to join her in a happily-ever-after fantasy of marriage and children. The poem reads in part:

> Oh, Hi-ho in the Lavender Woods
> A Sterile Cuckoo is crying;
> Oh, Hi-ho in the Lavender Snow,
> A Sterile Cuckoo is dying.
> Cuckoo! Cuckoo!
> Cuckoo! Cuckoo![29]

Part lament, part confession, part literary show-off (she cribs a line from F. Scott Fitzgerald to close the poem), these lines also use the repetition of the word 'cuckoo' to recall the relentless calling of the bird, like the swirling machinations of her restless mind and her own ceaseless chatter. Or is the 'Cuckoo!' coming from a clock, reminding these two not-yet-grown-up young adults that their time is running out?

Kesey and Nichols wrote with the cuckoo hovering over these dark comedies-cum-outright-tragedies, allowing it to suggest its full array of familiar associations: sexual desire and irresponsibility; seasonal comings and goings; irrationality and sudden twists of fate. But perhaps the best-known contemporary rendering of the crazy cuckoo takes a much lighter tack in the mascot Sonny the Cuckoo Bird, who has appeared in product branding and advertising for the General Mills breakfast cereal Cocoa Puffs (similar to Coco Pops in the UK) since the early 1960s. Sometimes Sonny is joined by 'Gramps'. Sonny becomes so excited whenever he sees a box of the cereal that he bounces off the wall and spins like a top, shedding feathers while his eyes turn into dizzying spirals, shrieking his signature line, 'I'm cuckoo for Cocoa Puffs!' Sonny doesn't bear any particular resemblance to a cuckoo, common or any other species. His yellow beak is outsized, toucan-like in scale but bulbous, and instead of the cuckoo's four toes, he has only three.

Instead of the common cuckoo's discreet browns and grey tones, Sonny is bright and solid orange or red. Even the sub-Saharan red-chested cuckoo, *Cuculus solitarius*, resembles its common cousin except for its rufous bib. Some couas, coucals and malkohas eschew the common cuckoo's neutral palette to sport green or blue plumages, but true oranges and reds are rare in the order. Red-faced malkohas, *Phaenicophaeus pyrrhocephalus*,

Cocoa Puffs 'throwback retro' design cereal boxes, c. 2015.

found in Sri Lanka, wear a kind of black-and-white tuxedo, with only a bright-red eye mask. As with many cartoon birds, most iterations of Sonny have him in clothing. Initially, when TV adverts were still filmed and aired in black and white, Sonny wore a vertically striped jacket, white shirt collar and black bow tie. Sometime in the 1960s, the jacket and tie gave way to a more hip pink-and-white striped turtleneck. In the 1990s, for a time, Sonny became a skateboarder, with loose shorts and kneepads. He eventually lost this costuming, but that hardly meant he took on a more naturalistic appearance. Still, some (but by no means all) versions of the advertisement for Cocoa Puffs end with a quick two-note rendering of the bird's notable song.[30]

In a classic early advert, Sonny, trying to resist temptation, tries wearing a blindfold to keep himself from seeing the sweet cereal, but, catching its scent, he loses all willpower, darts around rooms and levitates to the point of near explosion. In other versions of the TV advertisement, he chains himself up, hides in a cardboard box, confines himself to an elevator, locks the cereal box in a safe and even boards a rocket headed for outer space. Nothing works. The mere thought of his favourite food, or any remote suggestion of anything crunchy or chocolatey, would always send him into a spasmodic ecstasy without an iota of self-control.

Some observers have found the cuckoo not only daft but dense. Even the otherwise cuckoo-friendly naturalist James Hardy couldn't help himself:

Guira cuckoo (*Guira guira*) mother and three chicks.

Young cuckoos are stupid creatures and ill adapted to take care of themselves as pets. I am told of one brought up on porridge that got scalded to death, from flying into the pot newly off the fire, thus perishing amongst what it most sought after.[31]

Is that not often the way? One might instead question the intelligence of someone who tries to hold captive a wild animal, especially one whose instinct for migration is strong.

Decades later, another esteemed naturalist, Gerald Durrell, copped a similar attitude towards one of the cuckoo's cousins. On a trip to Argentina, collecting animals for London Zoo, he couldn't resist diagnosing the guira, a member of the cuckoo family, after a pair of fledglings was delivered to him:

I am convinced that they are mentally defective from the moment of hatching, and nothing will make me alter my opinion. As I lifted the lid from the box, it disclosed two guiras squatting straddle-legged in the bottom of the box, long tails spread out, and ginger crests erect. They surveyed me calmly with pale yellow eyes that had a glazed, dreamy, far-away expression in them, as though they were listening to distant and heavenly music too faint for mere mammals like myself to hear.[32]

What seems to have bothered Durrell most is that the fledglings appear to have had no fear of humans. They fluttered out of the box and landed on him to inspect his buttons, hair and ears. From another angle, we might call the birds curious. They perched readily on his wrist, and even if they proved comically clumsy and incessantly vocal, they happily received pets and scratches from Durrell's wife, Jacquie, who refused to believe that the birds were not already tame and had only been caught within the hour. 'Quite definitely mental', Durrell declared.[33] They adapted easily to captivity (as if they had a choice), and, when left alone in their cages for even short periods, welcomed their human captors' return with 'joyful trills of greeting'.[34] Much to the Durrells' surprise, these two guiras appeared to remember them two months after being placed with London Zoo:

> Thinking that such brainless birds would by now have completely forgotten us, we approached their cage in the bird-house with mixed feelings . . . But no sooner had we joined the spectators than the cuckoos, who a moment before had been preening themselves on their perch, stared at us with bright, mad eyes, erected their crests in astonishment, and flew down to the wire with loud rattles of excitement and pleasures. As we scratched their necks and watched them stretch out like rubber, we decided that perhaps they were not quite so unintelligent as we had supposed them to be.[35]

So much for Durrell's claim that nothing could alter his first impression of the guiras, which he met with the soft bigotry of low expectations.

Still, in many attempts by humans to differentiate ourselves from non-human animals by diminishing their cognitive powers, metaphors have a way of turning the tables on us. In the early twentieth century, John Edward Field, vicar of St Helen's Church in Benson, Oxfordshire, traced the 'myth of the pent cuckoo' to peculiar phenomena of the built and natural landscapes of the southern swathes of Britain, marked by tall stands of trees on raised ground.[36] This folk tale, collected in *The Merry Tales of the Wise Men of Gotham*, was first published in the sixteenth century

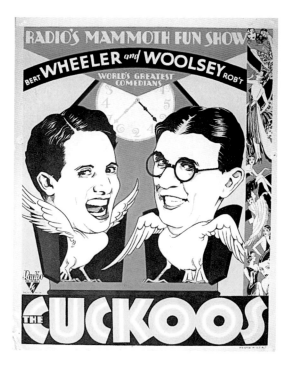

– but surely having circulated since the beginning of the second millennium – and goes like this:

> On a time the men of Gottam . . . made a hedge round in compasse, and they had got a Cuckoo, and had put her into it, and said, Sing here all the yeere, and thou shalt lack neither meat nor drinke. The Cuckoo as soon as she perceived her selfe incompassed within the hedge, flew away. A vengeance on her said they, We made not our hedge high enough.[37]

In another version of the tale, the men who believed so heartily that so long as the cuckoo was calling they would enjoy an endless summer 'had forgotten that it would learn to fly, and therefore they had not thought of roofing the enclosure'.[38] The cuckoo didn't forget. Who looks the fool now?

4 Nature's Timekeeper

'In Switzerland, they had brotherly love, they had
five hundred years of democracy and peace –
and what did that produce?
The cuckoo clock.'
Harry Lime in *The Third Man* (dir. Carol Reed, 1949)

Graham Greene once poked fun at the Swiss policy of political
neutrality in global affairs, but his geography was a little bit off.[1]
The cuckoo-clock actually originated in the early eighteenth century in what is now the German state of Baden-Württemberg. In
an authentic mechanical clock, the call of the cuckoo is produced
at intervals when two wooden chambers within the clock housing
fill with air, which is then expelled just as a door above the clock
face pops open and a small wooden bird emerges. The sound mimics one of the most distinctive, easily recognizable bird calls, the
male common cuckoo's two-note song. Modern adaptations might
substitute electronic quartz clocks for what in the original is a
mechanical marvel; they might drop Bavarian themes or play them
out to the point of kitsch; they might pare down the housing's
design to a simple bird box or an abstract variation. But the cuckoo
itself remains a staple feature of these timepieces. And why
shouldn't it? The common cuckoo's annual arrival in Europe has
long been received as the start of spring, warmly welcomed by
English Romantic poet William Wordsworth in 'To the Cuckoo':

O blithe New-comer! I have heard,
I hear thee and rejoice.
O Cuckoo! Shall I call thee Bird,
Or but a wandering Voice?

Adolphe Braun,
Canton d'Argovie,
c. 1869, albumen
silver print.

79

Wordsworth writes with reverence about the experience of hearing the first cuckoo of spring – and the cuckoo itself ('O blessed Bird!') – even if he never actually lay eyes on the notoriously elusive singer:

> To seek thee did I often rove
> Through woods and on the green;
> And thou wert still a hope, a love;
> Still longed for, never seen.[2]

Delightfully, he writes in the second person, directly to the cuckoo.

Although not everyone who hears their first cuckoo of spring has gone to the trouble of composing an eight-stanza poem, it is regarded as a sign so worth celebrating that *The Times* of London once published letters from readers claiming to have sighted the 'first cuckoo' of spring. So eager were some readers to leave winter behind that sometimes they got quite ahead of themselves. On 6 February 1913 *The Times* printed a letter written two days earlier by Richard Lydekker FRS (Fellow of the Royal Society), who reported that he and his 'under-gardener . . . both heard the full double note of a cuckoo repeated two or three times'. He admitted that they had not seen the bird. They only heard the song. Lydekker estimated the tune to have been sung at a distance of a quarter mile, but emphasized that 'there is not the slightest doubt that the song was that of a cuckoo'. Lydekker – naturalist, biogeologist, palaeontologist – certainly knew that this would be a bizarrely early date to find a cuckoo in England. He was, after, all, the author of numerous books of natural history, including *The Sportsman's British Bird Book* (1908). But he was not afraid to admit when he found himself in error. Six days later, on 12 February 1913, *The Times* published a follow-up letter in which Lydekker wrote:

I have been completely deceived in the matter of the supposed cuckoo of February 4. The note was uttered by a bricklayer's labourer at work on a house in the neighbourhood of the spot whence the note appeared to come. I have interviewed the man, who tells me that he is able to draw cuckoos from considerable distances by the exactness of his imitation of their notes, which he produces without the aid of any instrument.[3]

Anxious for one of the most dependable signs of spring to appear, even an expert could be fooled by a whistler who has mastered the cuckoo's simple song.

Cuckoo from *Birds of America* series for Allen & Ginter Cigarette Brands.

Decades later, other writers would skewer the Anglocentric
angle of the 'first cuckoo' letters. On 4 June 1977 David Mallon,
then affiliated with Mongolian State University, wrote to *The Times*
with marked brevity: 'Sir, I heard today the first cuckoo of the
year. Is this a record for Outer Mongolia?'[4] Again, the writer was
no casual observer. Mallon, now affiliated with Manchester

Metropolitan University and a member of the International Union for Conservation of Nature (IUCN) Red List Committee, is a renowned expert on the fauna of Central Asia.

The common cuckoo's migration is monitored closely, not only by winter-weary Britons, but by scientists and birders alike. The British Trust for Ornithology (BTO) operates the Cuckoo Tracking Project, tagging birds with tiny devices that allow their long voyages to be monitored. State-of-the-art tags weigh only about 4 grams (0.1 oz) and are fuelled by solar-powered batteries that cycle between 10 hours' worth of location-based data transmission and 48 hours of recharging time. Almost all of the tagged cuckoos are male; the BTO tags only birds that meet a certain minimum weight to be sure that the weight of the tag does not pose a significant threat. Males tend to be a little bit larger than females – and they are easier to lure into nets.[5] Tagged cuckoos are given proper names. Their portraits, as well as reports on their migrations, grace the BTO website. The BTO emails these reports to its supporters.[6]

The BTO's chronicles of the 2022 annual cuckoo migration are informative nail-biters – will he make it this time or won't he? – and they reveal just how little time the European cuckoo actually spends in Europe. Just a few days after the new year, the BTO reported that some seven tagged cuckoos had already begun flying north, leaving their winter homes in Gabon, the Republic of Congo, the Democratic Republic of Congo and Angola to return to breeding grounds in the UK. Each tagged cuckoo is not only named but identified by the site at which it was tagged. The cuckoo PJ, for example, who was tagged in Suffolk in 2016, spent the winter of 2022 in Gabon, but by March had flown northwest to Ghana and on to Ivory Coast, where he rested and fed for a few weeks before starting across the Sahara, following roughly the same route as in previous years. (Not that PJ was stuck in a rut;

sometimes his migration took a course closer to due north, entering Europe in northern Italy rather than southern Spain.) By early April, PJ made it to Spain, where he took another rest. On 24 or 25 April, PJ arrived in King's Forest, Suffolk, completing a round trip of just over 16,000 kilometres (10,000 mi.). This journey appears to have been his last. After six tracked years of migration – the most ever recorded – PJ would have been nearing the end of his natural lifespan. The BTO published one last report to honour the bird who, however unwittingly, provided researchers with a unique data set covering some 96,500 kilometres (60,000 mi.) and a dozen intercontinental flights.[7]

That might sound like a lot of airborne miles, but it isn't record-setting. In 2019–20, Onon, a tagged cuckoo, did an amazing 41,800-kilometre (26,000 mi.) round trip, from breeding grounds in Mongolia's Khurkh Valley to wintering grounds in southeastern Zambia and back again, in less than eleven months. Onon flew overland, following food sources, except for a long day of continuous flight over the Arabian Sea, departing Pakistan's southeastern coast just south of Karachi and regaining land on the easternmost tip of Oman, near Al Hadd. Onon left Mongolia again in July 2020, but researchers lost contact with the bird's signal late in September.[8]

Not all tagged cuckoos have such lengthy careers as research subjects. Charles was caught in a net and tagged at the Knepp Estate in West Sussex in May 2022. As May turned into June, he was already on his way south, crossing the English Channel and passing over the suburbs of Paris. By the end of June, Charles was flying in dry, hot conditions over Algeria. He was travelling at a good clip. At one point, the BTO reported that the bird covered 873 kilometres (543 mi.) in 26 hours, at a speed of almost 34 kilometres per hour (21 mph), despite mild headwinds. But the Saharan desert proved too much. Instead of continuing south as he crossed

Great spotted cuckoo (*Clamator glandarius*) on the wing. Like the common cuckoo, this species is a migratory brood parasite.

from Algeria into Mali, Charles turned west, apparently to avoid an unhospitable weather pattern. This detour kept Charles over the desert, rather than taking him more directly to more moderate climates and ample food and water. On 28 July 2022, the BTO reported that Charles was 'gone but not forgotten'.[9]

Still, not all the news is sad. Jac, tagged in 2021 in Llangollen on the River Dee in Wales, and Joe, tagged in Norfolk in 2022, reached their breeding grounds in April 2023. In spring 2023 BTO volunteers tagged ten additional cuckoos, including four from Ireland and two birds that had been caught before and still sported leg rings, even though they had lost their tags. They were refitted and released to migrate as usual and return more data to the BTO team. By early June, some of these cuckoos began their treks southwards, while some stragglers remained, still calling, as spring turned to summer.[10]

Given the regularity of the cuckoo's appearances and disappearances from the European continent, it should come as no surprise that once clockmakers got the idea to build hour-announcing birdsong into their devices, they chose the cuckoo.

No doubt, the cuckoo's arrival and a clock's hourly announcements
mark the passage of time at very different intervals: the cuckoo's
migration is an annual sign of seasonal change, while a clock that
chimes on the hour punctuates a smaller period of time, the day.
And yet, the reliable cuckoo is the star of the Black Forest clock.

Not that clockmakers had not tried to build birds into their creations previously. An earlier clock installed in the Cathédrale Notre-Dame de Strasbourg in the mid-fourteenth century contained what is believed to be one of the first working automata, a crowing cock. But, as cuckoo-clock expert Karl Kochmann has written, 'Imitating the call of the rooster was difficult . . . the call of the cuckoo was simple.'[11] Quail, trumpeter and flute clocks also had their moments, but the cuckoo became the most popular.[12]

Cuckoo-clocks emerge from a craft movement that brought together advancements in clock mechanisms and Black Forest woodworking resources. Clocks whose hands are controlled by a system of weights, gears and pulleys have been around since the fourteenth century, but they were then so large that they had to be housed in tall towers, often churches. By the time the sixteenth century turned into the seventeenth, innovations in metalworking allowed for clockmakers to scale down to sizes suitable for private homes, in what came to be known as 'long case' clocks, 'hall' clocks, 'coffin' clocks or 'grandfather' clocks. Still, these timepieces were large luxury items out of the reach of most people.

Farmers and loggers in the Black Forest, adept at woodworking, began making simple small clocks during long winter downtimes. Eventually, in the 1730s, the cuckoo-clock emerged to become a durable and popular design. Then as now, the Black Forest clock was about the size and shape of a bird box, though some large and elaborate clocks were and still are made. These clocks occupy wooden housing decorated with carved floral designs, hunting iconography and pastoral or carnivalesque scenes. Sometimes the most complicated versions incorporate automated figures such as dancers on a rotating platform. What they have in common is a carved pendulum, often in the shape of a leaf; dangling weights, usually iron, often in the shape of pine cones;

and a strike system triggering levers that pop open a small door, allowing a small wooden bird to emerge just as a pair of bellows releases air to produce the two-note call of the male common cuckoo. The weights hang from chains, which are actually the mechanism that 'winds' each clock. Generally, one weight controls the clock's timekeeping function, and a second weight the cuckoo bird and its little door. If there is a third weight – which

Thomas Rowlandson, *Mrs Cuckoo Assisting Her Spousey to Wind Up the Clock*, late 18th or early 19th century, pen and ink with watercolour on paper.

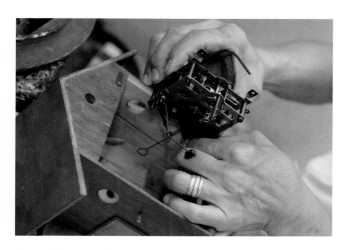

there often is in the more elaborate designs – it will drive the timing of additional moving or musical parts. To wind the clock, the user pulls a ring attached to one end of each chain until the pine-cone weight reaches the body of the clock. The weights will slowly descend, until they have dropped as far as they can, at which point the clock will stop. The chains are just under 2 metres, or 6 feet, long, so a cuckoo-clock must be hung fairly high on the wall. (Or one could follow Thomas Jefferson and cut a hole in the floor to let the weights drop to their full length if they would otherwise hit the floor.[13]) A one-day cuckoo-clock must be wound daily. An eight-day cuckoo-clock should be wound once each week. Variant designs, such as those in which the clock face is contained within a picture frame and adorned with a hand-painted scene, or spring-driven tabletop clocks, might jettison some of these features, but they all keep the cuckoo.

Black Forest clockmaking moved quickly from the individual craftworker's home to workshops and factories organized around assembly lines. Within a century, by around 1840, some half a

Making cuckoo-
clocks, Triberg,
in the Black Forest,
Germany, c. 1915,
stereograph.

million people were employed making these clocks, and produced
600,000 each year.[14] Most workers were men, specializing in one
component or another, but the little wooden cuckoos were often
made by women.[15] Not only did the clocks become more elabor-
ately ornamented, they branched out into new forms, with train
stations (a novelty in the mid-nineteenth century) or chalets
replacing the basic bird-box structure.

Tastes change. In 1965 the *New York Times* reported that while
there were 65 active cuckoo-clock factories in southwest Germany
before the Second World War, only sixteen then remained.[16] The
journalist attributed the flagging market to competition from
clock manufacturers in Switzerland and Japan, and noted that

few skilled artisans remained to hand-carve classic designs, and that the traditional linden wood, overharvested locally, now had to be imported. Likely, distaste for such recognizably German products after the war and the sleekness of mid-century design also began to chip away at the cuckoo-clock's popularity. Even in Germany, interest waned and its status fell: on a televised German game show, *Tick-Tack Quiz*, which was televised between 1958 and

The cuckoo and quail clock that hung in gangster Al Capone's office in the Lexington Hotel, Chicago, c. 1928–31.

1967, cuckoo-clocks played some role in set design, chiming when the episode was due to wrap up; more tellingly, the show offered cuckoo-clocks as consolation prizes to losers, never to winners.[17]

By contemporary standards, many of us would agree that a wall-hanging clock that has a complicated winding mechanism and sounds an alarm, no matter how naturalistically avian, might easily 'drive you cuckoo'.[18] Wordsworth, however, obviously fond of the living bird, seems to hold in his poem 'The Cuckoo-Clock' that its 'soft spontaneous note' can comfort the sleepless and prompt pleasant memories: 'Of sunshine wilt thou think, and flowers, and song./ And breathe as in a world where nothing can go wrong.' That is a lot of faith invested in not only the bird cuckoo but the cuckoo in the clock, to boot.

Cuckoo-clock aficionados persist, less poetically, perhaps, but at least as enthusiastically. In 1990 the clockmaking brothers Ramon and Max Pierkarski turned their private collection into the Cuckoo Clock Museum, now known as Cuckooland Museum, in Tabley, Cheshire.[19] Minneapolis, Minnesota, is home to the James J. Fiorentino Foundation and Museum, another private

Cuckoo-clock at Dove Cottage, where William Wordsworth lived from 1799 to 1808.

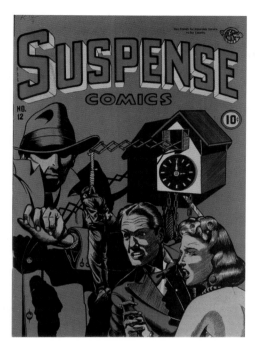

*Suspense
Comics*, no. 12
(10 September
1946).

collection that has opened to the public since 2007, featuring
not only cuckoo-clocks but hundreds of everyday household
objects. The German Clock Museum (Deutsches Uhrenmuseum)
in Furtwangen im Schwarzwald also started with a private collection, that of Robert Gerwig (1820–1885), who was the founding
director of that city's Clockmakers School. With a grand and
expansive collection focusing on Black Forest craftwork and
industry, the museum occupies a building which is part of Furtwangen University. In the small town of Sugarcreek, Ohio, a
7-metre-tall (23 ft) clock calls on the half-hour, paired with mechanical musicians and dancers who strike up a polka. Known as
the Little Switzerland of Ohio, and celebrating its history as home

Contender for the title of the world's largest cuckoo-clock, Sugarcreek, Ohio.

Contender for the title of world's largest cuckoo-clock, Wiesbaden.

to Swiss and German immigrants, Sugarcreek claims to have the world's largest cuckoo-clock. There are at least a dozen contenders for that title scattered as tourist attractions throughout Germany and elsewhere.[20]

Like many animals, the cuckoo appears in children's literature – as does the cuckoo-clock. In a Victorian novel for children by Mary Louisa Molesworth, writing simply as Mrs. Molesworth, the cuckoo in a prized cuckoo-clock is every bit as alive as a free-roaming bird. To the elderly aunties who share the grand old house, the clock is a good-luck talisman, a reminder of pleasant memories and, importantly, a standard-bearer for punctuality and 'faithful discharge of duty'.[21] After all, as a sign of the clock's quality, the little cuckoo never misses calling the hour, even when behind the clock face he might be very busy. Griselda, the young girl who comes to stay with these relatives, becomes fascinated with the clock, and eventually discovers that the cuckoo has a life of his own, inside the clock and out, and together they enjoy night-time adventures involving household artworks and knick-knacks that come to life, while the adults sleep unaware. The cuckoo is

Carved wooden cuckoo emerging from clock face.

even a wonderful singer, with a range far exceeding the two notes he delivers as clockwork.

Mrs. Molesworth lets the cuckoo become more than just a dependable cog in a machine, more than a harbinger of spring. But frequently literary cuckoos are not fully realized characters, only clues to relationships among characters, avian symbols without an avian presence. As often as not, authors draw on the association

of the cuckoo with irrational or outlandish behaviour, or as a swipe at a character's mental illness. In J. K. Rowling's mystery novel *The Cuckoo's Calling* (written under the pseudonym Robert Galbraith), a detective investigates the death of a troubled fashion model who wore 'Cuckoo' as a nickname. Likewise, the title character of the British sitcom *Cuckoo* is a ne'er-do-well free spirit who brings chaos to his girlfriend's family. Elsewhere, references to cuckoos in genre fiction – thrillers, science fiction, romance novels – often suggest that there will be a storyline about uncertain parentage. (In subsequent seasons of the *Cuckoo* television series, children and siblings that characters didn't know of previously pop up here and there, so the cuckoo title gets to do double duty.) In the twelve-part manga series *A Couple of Cuckoos* by Miki Yoshikawa, the protagonists, Nagi and Erika, were switched at birth at the hospital where they both were born. Learning the truth as adolescents, these 'cuckoo's eggs' discover that their parents intend for the two to marry, merging the families to make up for the hospital's error.

Plastic cuckoo emerging from a wooden clock.

The same device pops up in serious literature too. For example, in Emily Brontë's *Wuthering Heights*, the narrator, newly renting a property owned by the gruff and mysterious Mr Heathcliff, induces his housekeeper to tell the history of the land and his landlord. She begins with a famous line: 'It's a cuckoo's, sir.'[22] Heathcliff, of course, is adopted into the Earnshaw family, who are the land's previous owners. He is favoured by Mr Earnshaw, abused by an elder brother and passionately in love with his adoptive sister, Catherine, who eventually marries a man with a very different temperament. Only much later in the novel, as the complicated, deadly love triangle unfolds, does a cuckoo reappear, in a fantasy of Catherine's, in a chorus of 'not only larks, but throstles, and blackbirds, and linnets, and cuckoos pouring out music on every side', a reminder, perhaps, of her equivocating desire for both the refinement of Edgar Linton and the ferocity of Heathcliff.[23]

For all these metaphorical cuckoos, the bird must get back to the business of marking time. The cuckoo appears as a literal

Jack and unfriendly classmates, in the French animated film *Jack et la mécanique du coeur* (2013).

timekeeper in the novella *The Boy with the Cuckoo-Clock Heart* by Mathias Malzieu. A miniature cuckoo-clock becomes a sort of pacemaker that saves the life of Jack, a boy born on such a cold day in Edinburgh that his heart is frozen. The midwife who assists in his birth, who also happens to be a creative prosthetist (and possibly a witch), installs the device. The clock measures only about 4 × 8 centimetres (1.5 × 3 in.), and it is wound with a key rather than dependent on weights.[24] Its hands pass sharply through the boy's chest. True to form, the clock contains a tiny wooden bird that pops out to utter the cuckoo's call. The midwife warns Jack that as he grows up his heart will not be able to bear the strain of intense love or rage. But, of course, he experiences both strong emotions, putting himself in great peril – or, more accurately, believing himself to be in great peril.

Fortunately for the rest of us, our clocks stay firmly on the floor, the wall or the shelf. Well, a few entrepreneurs have attempted to bring cuckoo-clock sensibilities into wearable timepieces, with limited success. The Cookoo smartwatch hit the market in about 2013, with an analogue dial on its face and limited capacity to connect to a smartphone and provide the user with notifications, but the product line seems to have been abandoned within a few years. The cutely spelled name was just a gimmick, anyway; no birdsong was involved. Around 2021, a designer named Kiyotaka Akasaka built a real miniature cuckoo-clock, with digital components inside a wooden housing, complete with a tiny bird that pops out and calls on the hour. Bulkier than a normal wristwatch (but just about the size of the clock-heart worn by Jack), this project appears to have been a labour of singular love.[25]

I remember growing up with a cuckoo-clock in the house, in a small city in the U.S. Midwest. Hung high on a living-room wall, the clock seemed oddly exotic. It was a 'mustn't touch' object, and only my father knew how to keep it running. Somewhere along

the line, he must have stopped keeping up with it, because I don't remember the cuckoo calling much. It was a classic but very simple design, about the size of a bird box with a pitched roof, adorned with five carved maple leaves and a carved bird perched on the roof's apex. I recently pulled it from a clutter of bric-a-brac destined for a local charity shop. Family lore suggests that it might have previously belonged to my paternal grandfather.[26] If, to a child, the clock seemed a bit foreign, mysterious and out of place, now it's a shabby, fragile relic with a crack in the roof, a missing pendulum and only about half of the clock face's Roman numerals still in place. But pop off the back of the housing to reveal the clock's inner workings and fiddle a bit with a couple of levers, and a minor mechanical miracle occurs: on the front side a little door opens, and a bird peeks out as paper bellows inside the box toot the familiar song.

A cuckoo-clock that belonged to the author's father, a little worse for wear.

Shown in reverse, exposing the bellows and movement.

5   The Cuckoo's Song

'When he got to the middle of the room, the cuckoo cleared his throat, flapped his wings, and began to sing. Griselda was quite astonished. She had had no idea that her friend was so accomplished. It wasn't "cuckooing" at all; it was real singing, like that of the nightingale or the thrush, or like something prettier than either.'
From *The Cuckoo Clock* by Mrs Molesworth (1877)

The common cuckoo's song is one of the most recognizable bird calls, familiar even to many who have never seen a cuckoo in the wild. The two-note song of the male common cuckoo is the sound from which is derived the two-syllable sound-alike name of the bird. It isn't complex and variable, like the songs of the nightingale and thrush, and whether the cuckoo's call is even half as pretty as those other birds' is a matter of opinion. Still, music lovers and some of the most prominent composers have found musicality in the cuckoo's simple song.

One especially keen listener, Margaret A. Barrett of Neston, Cheshire, took it upon herself to write to the journal the *Musical Times* in 1897 to clear up some previously published confusion about the cuckoo's song. She describes the typical spring call as a minor third, based on the interval of three half-steps between the notes. Come summer, however, the pitch of the notes may change (recall lines from the old rhyme, 'The cuckoo . . . sings a song in May/ Then in June another tune'), taking the form of a major third. A musician friend affirmed that a late summer recording of a cuckoo calling took this form, transcribing the initial note as an E, followed by a C. As summer wears on, the tune shifts to a major fourth or fifth.[1] Then, 'in June, out of tune, she [*sic*] cannot sing a note,' the saying goes.[2] No need to sing

Barbara Regina Dietzsch, 'Grauer Kukuk', from *Sammlung meistens Deutscher Vogel* (Collection of Mostly German Birds, 1772–7), handcoloured folio engraving.

anyway, as the cuckoo turns his focus from the mating game to migration.

The male common cuckoo not only sings the two-note song. That's just his signature tune, echoed widely as the model for humans' household doorbells – and, of course, for the cuckoo-clock. He might call out two notes to let everyone nearby know he is there, but once a female responds, he may switch to a three-note arrangement. (There are many ways of phonetically transcribing birdsong. Let 'cu-coo' and 'ci-cu-coo' suffice here.) This behaviour is not easy to observe. After all, cuckoos themselves are not easily observed, with their cryptic plumage and tendency to hide in foliage rather than settle on visible perches. When Mark E. Hauber and Csaba Moskát set out to study how the cuckoo uses his different vocalizations, they recorded instances of cuckoos calling each May from 2016 to 2020 at a site in central Hungary where cuckoos breed, parasitizing reed-warbler nests. They demonstrated that the male almost never adds the third note unless he is in very close proximity to a female, and about two-thirds of the time, the female initiates the conversation. While these exchanges tended not to last long in the study (rarely did the females repeat themselves, while the males tended to call two or three times once they started), they are evidence of the sexes using their voices cooperatively as part of their courting ritual or territorial defence.[3] This phenomenon is known as duetting, and it is fairly common among birds that pair-bond for any length of time, a season or a lifetime – less so among those whose liaisons, like the cuckoo's, are more fleeting.

An adult male's *cu-coo* is a repetitive call, but rather gentle. Young common cuckoos vocalize differently. The Anglican curate Gilbert White, a naturalist who meticulously observed the flora and fauna of Selborne, a village in Hampshire, in the south of England, wrote in the 1780s that the young cuckoo's cry is 'very peculiar . . . plaintive . . . a wonderful provision to attract soft-billed birds to feed the helpless cuckoo in its foster-mother's nest'.[4] More bluntly, a wildlife rehabilitator who tended an orphaned common-cuckoo chick until it could be released to the wild described its voice as 'a car alarm blended with a whistling kettle', as insistent as its seemingly insatiable appetite.[5] Perhaps we should count ourselves lucky that few of us will ever get to hear the cuckoo nestling's demanding call. Of course, the young cuckoo's mother never hears its screech either.

For their part, females make a different sound, which is most often described as 'bubbling', 'a chuckle' or 'like bathwater gurgling down a plug hole'.[6] It's hard to accurately spell out the call, though it is often given as '*kwik-kwik-kwik*'.[7] It is well known that the common cuckoo's appearance mimics the sparrowhawk's, which may help to scare the passerines that the cuckoo seeks to parasitize, shooing them away from their nests long enough for the interloping egg to be laid and left behind. Doing so requires a combination of stealth – acting quickly and avoiding detection – and deception – faking out the host who gets a glimpse of the cuckoo and knows what she's up to. If a host realizes that a cuckoo might have designs on their nest, they might try 'mobbing' to chase her away, and if they have good reason to suspect that a cuckoo has made it through their defences and deposited an egg next to their own, their chance of recognizing the interloper and rejecting it increases. Nevertheless, quite counterintuitively (at least to this human's logic), female cuckoos do call in the vicinity of a host nest, and often do so just after laying an egg, which the ornithologist Edgar Percival Chance observed during his famous studies at Wicken Fen, near Cambridge, between 1918 and 1925.[8] He also recorded another type of vocalization by the female, described as 'mewing', while she waited for her opportunity to slip an egg into a meadow pipit's nest.[9]

One might think that calling would reduce a parasitic bird's success, since it would announce her presence. Instead, the call

Edgar Percival Chance and friends, entering a hide from which to observe cuckoos at Wicken Fen.

Wicken Fen remains
a noted cuckoo
breeding ground.

turns out to be another tool she uses to distract and deceive
potential hosts. Just as her plumage recalls a predatory sparrowhawk, so too does her song. An experienced human can discern
one from another; to a breeding songbird, the similarities are
too worrisome to take the risk.[10] Nearly a century after Chance
observed the cuckoos of Wicken Fen, Jenny E. York and Nick
Davies tested how reed warblers responded to various calls in and
around the same terrain. The warblers largely ignored the male's
cu-coo and a dove's *coo*, as expected. They pose no direct threat
to either host or clutch. But both the sparrowhawk and female-
cuckoo recordings prompted the warblers to 'become vigilant'
and distracted from their own clutch. The sparrowhawk, after
all, has little interest in the eggs, but will prey on warblers, so
protecting themselves, rather than their unhatched eggs, became
job number one. Accordingly, the chance of parasitism increases
and the likelihood that the interloping egg will be rejected

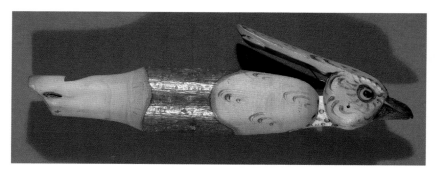

decreases.[11] While York and Davies avoided judging the cuckoo's reproductive strategies as naughty or nice, a précis in the esteemed journal *Nature* went all out, calling the vocal mimicry (or, at least, similarity) 'a dark twist' and declaring that the 'female of the species is sneakier than the male . . . [she] does the actual dirty work'.[12] Other science writers have been even more blunt: 'Cuckoos are even bigger assholes than we realized.'[13] The human impulse to moralize proves, once again, hard to resist.

Other members of the order to which the common cuckoo belongs can make a wide range of noises. Black-billed cuckoos (*Coccyzus erythropthalmus*), for example, can sound at times like a burping frog or a telephone's busy signal; they breed in the central and eastern USA and in parts of Canada, wintering in Colombia, Peru and Bolivia. The yellow-billed cuckoo (*Coccyzus americanus*), whose range is similar to that of the black-billed but sprawls over Brazil in winter, calls a surprised '*Oh! Oh! Oh!*'. Nicknamed the 'rain crow' or 'storm crow', it is not afraid to call when thunder cracks. The mangrove cuckoo (*Coccyzus minor*), a year-round resident of coastal Central America and the Caribbean islands, erupts in a series of short squawks. The channel-billed cuckoo (*Scythrops novaehollandiae*), a big Australian bird with bright-red eyes, is monstrously loud.[14] The common hawk cuckoo of India (*Hierococcyx varius*), which resembles the shikra or little banded goshawk (*Accipiter badius*) just as the common cuckoo resembles the sparrowhawk, is sometimes called the 'brain-fever bird'. Its rapid three-note call grows increasingly loud as it is repeated and goes on through day and night, rather desperately. It might take some imagination to transcribe the call as some do: '*brain fever, brain fever, BRAIN-FEVER*'. The alternatives in Hindi and in Marathi – '*piya-kaha*' ('where is the beloved') and '*paos-ala*' ('rain is coming'), respectively – provide less maddening alternatives.[15]

Composers, at least those in Western traditions, who are inspired by the cuckoo's song usually go for the gentler sound of the common cuckoo, finding it most suitable for welcoming the arrival

Mangrove cuckoo.

of springtime or simply celebrating birdsong. Among works by too many cuckoo-inspired classical composers to explore here, Antonio Vivaldi is prominent, drawing on the cuckoo's song in both his Violin Concerto in A major (RV 335, 'The Cuckoo'), published in 1716, and in Concerto No. 2 in G Minor (RV 315), otherwise very well-known as the 'Summer' section of his *Four Seasons*, first published in 1725. His literalization of sounds from nature

Ogata Gekko, *Cuckoo with Full Moon*, c. 1890–1910, colour woodblock print on paper.

Sheet music for
J. E. Magruder,
'Cuckoo March',
1879.

was then considered innovative. Both are bright, evocative and much-loved compositions.

The cuckoo is often paired with the nightingale, a bird whose migratory path is not dissimilar, and who is every bit as much a harbinger of spring in Western and Central Europe and elsewhere.[16] In Handel's Organ Concerto in F Major, known as 'The Cuckoo and the Nightingale' (1739), an organist introduces the cuckoo with their right hand and then adds the left to bring in the more complex nightingale song. Gustav Mahler made the same pairing over and over, in 'Lob des hohen Verstandes' ('In Praise of Lofty Intellect') and in 'Ablösung im Sommer' ('The

Changing of the Guard in Summer', 1888–9), from the song cycle *Des Knaben Wunderhorn* ('The Boy's Magic Horn', 1905) which set folk-tales to music. The former uses birdsong to comic effect; the latter is melancholic, with the death of the cuckoo setting the stage for the nightingale's song to dominate the scene.[17]

The call of the cuckoo is heard in an equally sober section of Camille Saint-Saëns' mostly playful *Carnival of the Animals*, composed in 1886. Saint-Saëns permitted the suite to be played only in a few private concerts during his lifetime. Ironically, once published and performed publicly in 1922, it became one of his most recognized and popular works, if uncharacteristically light-hearted. The piece shifts tone constantly throughout its fourteen movements. Preceded by a very short movement, 'Characters with Long Ears', in which violins bray like donkeys, and followed by 'Aviary', a cheerful, chattering number, 'The Cuckoo in the Depth of the Woods' is sombre. The score called for the cuckoo to be played as a C followed by an A flat – perhaps oddly, since that sequence is the minor sixth interval that others have said the cuckoo just can't reach – but it does capture the plaintive quality of the call. Written for two pianos and clarinet, and at about two and three-quarter minutes, this is one of the *Carnival*'s longer movements. The pianos appear to play the role of the forest's trees, stolid and serious. Typically, the clarinet playing the notes of the cuckoo in this piece is offstage, adding a spatial dimension that recalls that the bird, being a bit secretive, may be more easily heard from a distance than sighted.[18]

A clarinet often stands in for the cuckoo in classical music, as it did for Saint-Saëns, and as it did earlier for Ludwig van Beethoven in his Symphony No. 6 in F major (Op. 68, 1808), known as his *Pastoral Symphony*. If the *Carnival of the Animals* is an eclectic menagerie, the *Pastoral* is a grand, even grandiose, walk in the woods. Like a landscape painting transformed into music, the piece follows the ramblings of a babbling brook and captures birdsong, a thunderstorm, a shepherd's flute and other rural soundscapes. While critics have quibbled, in Beethoven's lifetime and afterwards, about whether this kind of sonic realism is the best work of such an esteemed composer, there's no denying its pleasure, a sort of contemplative gentility that doesn't entirely overtake bolder moments.[19] At the end of the second movement, known as 'Scene by the Brook', the voices of three birds are unmistakable: the flute/nightingale, the oboe/quail and the clarinet (two, actually) for the cuckoo. Beethoven may have bristled at the suggestion that this was all a bit of a joke: at least one analysis of the movement pays plenty of mind to the unmistakable nature sounds, but also finds a rueful allegory of Beethoven's oncoming deafness as the scene fades.[20]

But of course, the cuckoo is more than just a harbinger of spring, and it plays other roles in non-classical genres. The cuckoo's association with fleeting or unfaithful love surfaces in some versions of

Pair of cuckoos, Chelsea Porcelain Manufactory, soft-paste porcelain, c. 1750.

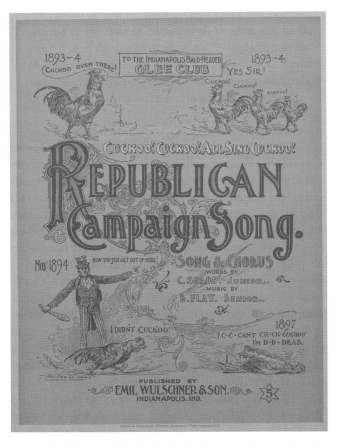

Sheet music for B. Flat Senior and C. Sharp Junior (pseudonyms), 'Cuckoo! Cuckoo! All Sing Cuckoo!', 1894. This was a Republican campaign song ridiculing the administration of U.S. President Grover Cleveland.

the English folk song 'The Cuckoo', which dates at least to the early nineteenth century and probably much earlier, with close Irish, Scottish, Canadian and U.S. variants. James Hardy's 1879 'Popular History of the Cuckoo' reproduces multiple versions from William Howitt's *The Book of the Seasons*; given that this source was first published in 1831, it's likely that the tune pre-dates its first publication, which was in undated broadsheets roughly circa 1800.[21] The exact lyrics change frequently but are set to the same tune: 'The cuckoo comes in April', 'The cuckoo is a fine bird', 'In April I open my bill' and 'The cuckoo is a pretty bird' serve as opening lines, among many others. The first recording of the song was by country singer Kelly Harrell in 1926, and dozens of other recordings have followed. For example, Bob Dylan played the song live at a Greenwich Village nightclub in 1962, a performance released in 2005 on the album *Live at the Gaslight 1962*, and many other folk singers followed suit, but the song also found its way into other genres. The blues musician Taj Mahal put out a sultry, intimate recording in 1968. Big Brother and the Holding Company featuring Janis Joplin recorded a fast-charging version, shrewd

Flora Wallace, *Cuckoo*, c. 2020, artwork for the song 'Cuckoo' by Cosmo Sheldrake on the album *Wake Up Calls* (2020).

and anguished in tone; both work in warnings about the fate of a gambling man and hints of a woman taking wing. Some of these modern adaptations don't quite get the bird at the song's core right, in favour of the rhyming structure, claiming that the bird appears only on the fourth of July, which would be awfully late. British 'folktronica' musician Cosmo Sheldrake incorporates recorded birdsong into his lovely 'Cuckoo Song', a modern version that returns its focus to the bird, leaving human broken hearts out of it.

Elsewhere, the cuckoo's association with nagging household clocks is immortalized in pop songs. Legendary lyricist Johnny Mercer penned 'Cuckoo in the Clock', a bouncy ditty composed by Walter Donaldson and first recorded in 1939 by the playful big-band leader Kay Kyser and his orchestra, with vocals by Sully Mason. The original record substituted a tooting kazoo for the

James Heath, after James Bruce, *Bee Cuckoo*, 1790, engraving.

Cuckoo, from Rev. F. O. Morris, *Bible Natural History; Containing a Description of Quadrupeds, Birds, Trees, Plants, Insects, Etc., Mentioned in The Holy Scriptures* (1856).

cuckoo's call. Another 1939 recording, by Mercer himself, gets some of its cuckoo calls from Benny Goodman's clarinet. Others who tried the tune, such as Lena Horne, who recorded 'Cuckoo in the Clock' for her 1963 samba-infused album *Lena Like Latin*, were game to rely on their own voices for the bird's lines. In the song, a man has set about lavishing flattery on the object of his affections. The little bird emerging on the quarter hour from a nearby cuckoo-clock may occasionally disrupt the romantic scene, but the young couple appears to be oblivious that the cuckoo is actually observing and eavesdropping on them. A performer blows a juicy 'raspberry' – the flatulent sound produced by fluttering one's lips and tongue together – to express the cuckoo's disapproval of the scene, though it is uncertain whether the bird disdains the couple's

Stuffed toy that makes a realistic cuckoo call when squeezed.

canoodling or just the man's corny patter and clumsy attempt at seduction.

A cuckoo-clock calling every fifteen minutes, as in 'The Cuckoo in the Clock', suggests a mood-spoiling annoyance. The Beach Boys' 'Cuckoo Clock' took the trope of the clock's incessant, insistent chime a step further.[22] In this song, written by Brian Wilson and Gary Usher and included on the album *Surfin' Safari* (1962), the young lovers seem all too aware of the passage of time. The group uses its famous harmonizing to keep up a 'tick-tock' refrain under Wilson's lead vocals. The singer reports that he first shoos away the noisy bird, then eventually destroys it. Legend has it that a myna, kept as a pet by Brian Wilson's father, inspired the song. Transforming the bird into a cuckoo to exploit its association with timekeeping adds an urgency to the tryst, however lightweight the song.

As easy as it may seem to reproduce the call of the male cuckoo (the female's call is quite a bit trickier), it may not be a good idea. As an unnamed man belonging to the Ainu ethnic group of Japan and Russia told missionary John Batchelor around the turn of the twentieth century:

> There are five birds that should never be imitated by anyone. They are the cuckoo, woodpecker, nighthawk, goatsucker, and owl. These birds have the power to bewitch people by means of their cry, and sometimes do so. Their cry ought therefore not to be imitated. To do so, indeed, would be a direct calling in of misfortune.[23]

Have we brought bad luck on ourselves – or on the cuckoo – by trying so hard to replicate its voice, to sing its song as if it were our own? While this writer is in no position to question Ainu mythology, I suspect that it has been other human activities, not so much our musical efforts, that put the cuckoo at risk, as we will see in the next chapter.

BIRDS' NESTS, EGGS & EGG-COLLECTING

RICHARD KEARTON
F. Z. S.

6 Cuckoo Futures

'"You're cuckoo!" my friends shouted at me. But what the cuckoo was exactly, I still didn't know. The cuckoo was a feeling, a surmise, a gallimaufry of birds, a none-such, that lived high in the branches of a tree in a nest of sticks and peered vaguely down at the surrounding world, occasionally uttering a mad, bisyllabic cry that unsettled my brain.'
George Scarborough, 1965[1]

What is the future of the cuckoo? Modern science has done a fine job of discounting some myths that even Aristotle and Pliny the Elder failed to shake: the cuckoo is a cuckoo, the hawk is a hawk, and neither is a seasonal changeling. In Shakespeare's day (and well beyond it), when the Church and the monarchy kept in place tight social strictures, the cuckoo and its linguistic offspring, the cuckold, did hard labour reminding readers and playgoers that marital fidelity is a virtue – and that paternity is a source of both anxiety and power. In a liberalizing world of commonplace no-fault divorce, serial monogamy, blended and queer families and other non-traditional social formations (as well as the diminishing role of inherited royalty), 'cuckold' sounds more than a bit archaic, even as it morphs into the reactionary insult 'cuck'. Pop, rap, R&B and hip-hop musicians of the late twentieth and early twenty-first centuries may not call on birdsong melodically as much as some of their classical forerunners did, but they are keeping alive the use of 'cuckoo' as a term for someone gone bonkers: The Breeders' 'Cannonball' (1993), Mavis Staples's 'Last Train' (2010), 'The Monster' by Eminem featuring Rihanna (2013), Animal Collective's 'Cuckoo Cuckoo' (2007), Rihanna's 'Cockiness (Love It) Remix' featuring A$AP Rocky (2011) preserve both that meaning and a more obscure use of 'cuckoo' as a slang term for

Alison Stockmarr, *Birds Nests, Eggs and Egg-Collecting*, 2019, giclée print of collaged book work.

Common cuckoo
eating a grub.

sex organs. Jim Jones's 'Supa Hot (Remix)' featuring Nicki Minaj
and Sonny Rich (2009) even works in homage to the sugary-
cereal buff Sonny the Cuckoo Bird. The bird itself may be reced-
ing from these usages, but at least some of the metaphors it has
inspired live on.

And what about the birds themselves, metaphors and myths
and rhymes aside? From one wide angle, the many species of
cuckoo, taken as a whole, may be doing all right. The IUCN lists
the vast majority of cuckoo species as of 'least concern'.[2] The
common cuckoo itself (*Cuculus canorus*) is among them, despite
evidence that the population is declining, at least in Europe,
where the most data is collected. Still, with a breeding-season
population estimated at 11.9 to 21.5 million adult cuckoos, and
at least 40 million and perhaps as many as 75 million common
cuckoos worldwide, there may be little reason to be alarmed.[3] But
that hardly means that the species is not facing real challenges,
primarily due to anthropogenic climate change.

In 2009 a coalition of British conservationist organizations
added the cuckoo to its *Birds of Conservation Concern* red list, its

designation for species most urgently in need of protection. The British Trust for Ornithology's (BTO) *Breeding Bird Survey* issued in 2022 indicated that the cuckoo population declined some 36 per cent between 1995 and 2021. Isolating England from the rest of the UK, that decline is an astonishing 76 per cent over the same 26-year period.[4] Given the rich roles it has played in the region's folklore and literature, from Chaucer to Shakespeare and beyond,

Brochure promoting the Cuckoo Trail, East Sussex.

it's no wonder that there is avid interest in the fate of this iconic seasonal visitor to the UK.

One cause of the declining UK cuckoo population seems to be a migration route that is growing ever more challenging. Researchers affiliated with the BTO, led by Chris Hewson, compared mortality rates between cuckoos taking the 'west route' to their winter homes in Central Africa, via Spain prior to crossing the Sahara, with those taking the 'east route' through Italy or the Balkans. Surprisingly, they found that even though the west route is shorter, it produced more fatalities in Europe prior to the desert crossing, due at least in part to drought and wildfires in Spain during the years that data was collected, 2011–14.[5]

Another changing constraint on the cuckoo is its dependence on other birds, most of which are migratory, who serve as hosts for its eggs. Songbirds – potential cuckoo hosts – lay one egg per day, until four to six eggs are in the nest. The cuckoo, in contrast, lays only every two or three days, and can lay ten, fifteen, even twenty or more eggs during one breeding season.[6] That way, she has time to exploit the nests of both early and late-laying hosts. But many hosts that migrate are shifting the timing of their migrations and their breeding seasons in response to a warming climate. Meanwhile, the cuckoo has barely changed its routine, leaving its winter home and its breeding grounds at almost exactly the same time year after year. If host and parasite breeding cycles fall out of sync, the cuckoo may find fewer opportunities to place her eggs in a nest where it is similar enough to the host eggs to be accepted, which would negatively impact reproductive success.[7] And, of course, declines in any host population would leave the cuckoo that parasitizes its nests without good options. While some typical hosts are thriving, others have declined sharply over the period 1995–2022: the sedge warbler, down 19 per cent; the linnet, down 23 per cent; the greenfinch, down 68 per cent.[8]

Katsushika Hokusai, *Cuckoo and Azaleas*, 1829–39, colour woodblock print.

124

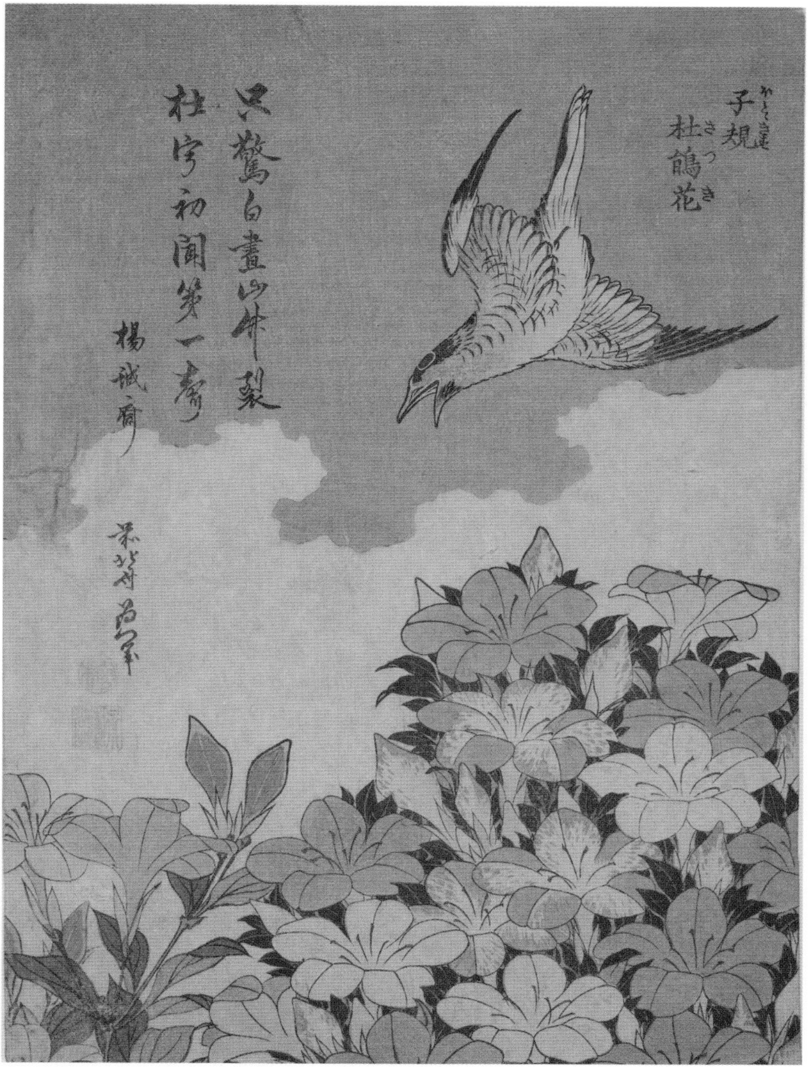

ほとゝぎす
子規
さつき
杜鵑花
只驚白晝山中裂
杜宇初聞第一聲
楊誠斎
前北斎為一筆

Annie Harnett,
Cuckoo, 2022,
mixed media
drawing.

John Gould,
Cuculus canorus,
from *The Birds of
Great Britain*, vol.
III (1873).

In its westernmost European breeding grounds and migratory routes, then, cuckoos are struggling under these climate-impacted conditions. On the other, far eastern edge of Eurasia, another kind of change is afoot. Not so long ago, the common cuckoo, confined to the Eastern Hemisphere, bred no further east than Siberia. Now, common cuckoos and oriental cuckoos (*Cuculus optatus*) have crossed over the Bering Strait into Alaska. Though no one is yet certain of their numbers, it is likely that they have begun to breed and to move into parts of Canada. By 2012 at least one common cuckoo was spotted in central California, and evidence is accruing to suggest that it has not been the only one of its kind to venture through the state.[9] A good move, perhaps, for the cuckoos, who may be responding to climate change and fluctuating food supplies by following their noses to hospitable environs with rich food sources during the season when they need to fatten up in preparation for migration. But what impact will this have on other birds? Recent scientific studies suggest that the cuckoo's arrival in North America may take a toll on the continent's native bird populations.

Since both common and oriental cuckoos are obligate brood parasites, if they move into new territories, they must find new hosts in whose nests they can lay their eggs. North America already has its own brood parasites; for example, the brown-headed cowbird is distributed throughout most of the continental USA as well as the western provinces of Canada. The cowbird's territory is expanding northwards, but doesn't quite reach the most northern and western parts of Alaska, where the cuckoos are gaining footholds. The cuckoos will find that some potential hosts in Alaska have little or no prior experience with brood parasites, and therefore have not developed defences against it. Researchers have conducted experiments to test how these species might interact, and the news was not great. Even the American robin, which is quite expert at discerning the presence of cowbird eggs and removing them from the nest, failed to reject model cuckoo eggs placed in their nests.[10]

This is not the only advantage that the cuckoos have. Cuckoo chicks have powerful ways of monopolizing their foster parents' attention. While cowbird hatchlings typically do not kick their host's offspring out of the nest, common and oriental cuckoo hatchlings almost always remove their competition, ensuring that they will receive all of the food the host parents can deliver without having to share with siblings. In doing so, they reduce the host's reproductive rate, suggesting that North American songbirds may suffer if the cuckoo thrives.[11]

What about the cuckoo family, *Cuculidae*, as a whole? Fortunately, there are but two extinctions recorded by the leading

Horsfield's cuckoo (also known as the oriental cuckoo, *Cuculus optatus*).

international conservation groups in the modern era.[12] The snail-eating or Delalande's coua (*Coua delalandei*), once endemic to the island of Nosy Boraha off the eastern coast of Madagascar, is thought to be extinct. Its decline was caused by habitat loss, hunting and competition or predation by introduced species.[13] Sources differ on whether the last known museum specimen was collected in 1834 or as late as 1850.[14] Reports of later sightings have been largely discounted. Relatively large, measuring around 56 centimetres (22 in.) in length, this bird had iridescent indigo or purple feathers and lived on snails, cracking the shells against a stone, like an anvil, to get to their meat.

At only 15–18 centimetres (5.9–7 in.) in length, the St Helena cuckoo (*Nannococcyx psix*) was one of the smallest cuckoos. It was driven to extinction sometime in the eighteenth century. Its sole habitat, the island of St Helena in the South Atlantic Ocean, part of a British Overseas Territory which includes Ascension and Tristan da Cunha islands, was uninhabited when Portuguese sailors discovered it in 1502. The island was established as a port of call for ships crossing the Atlantic engaged in slave-trading, including the Dutch and British East India Companies. Colonialism and agriculture (itself sustained by slave labour) remade its tropical forests into farmland inhospitable to native fauna like the St Helena cuckoo.

While the IUCN Red List categorizes most species of cuckoos, coucals, couas, malkohas and their close kin as of 'least concern',

Common cuckoo, Natural History Museum, Colchester, Essex, UK.

some members of this animal family are increasingly recognized as threatened. The red-faced malkoha (*Phaenicophaeus pyrrhocephalus*) has been red-listed as 'vulnerable' by the IUCN since 1994, as its habitat in the lowland forests of Sri Lanka has been degraded by logging and mining.[15] The coral-billed ground cuckoo (*Carpococcyx renauldi*) was designated 'vulnerable' in 2018 after decades of little concern, due to 'hunting pressure and habitat

Cuckoo: A Society Game (trademark document), 1891.

Gustav Mützel's illustration of a yellow-billed cuckoo, from Richard Lydekker's *The Royal Natural History*, vol. IV: *Birds* (1895).

loss', especially in Vietnam and Laos.[16] In 2022 the status of the Bornean ground cuckoo (*Carpococcyx radiceus*) was changed from 'near threatened' to the more serious 'vulnerable' in light of a population decline of at least 40 per cent over ten years, due largely to deforestation resulting from the rapid expansion of palm-oil factories.[17]

At least one cuckoo species is in an even graver situation. Since the year 2000, the bay-breasted (or rufous-breasted) cuckoo (*Coccyzus rufigularis*) has been listed as 'endangered'. Its habitat has shrunk to two small zones on the island of Hispaniola, mostly in the Dominican Republic. Some estimates of the surviving population are in the low hundreds. The conversion of forests to grazing land, hunting and possibly the impact of chemicals used in agriculture are to blame.[18]

International non-governmental agencies are not the only entities charged with identifying threatened populations and

A cuckoo appears in *RRR* (dir. S. S. Rajamouli, 2022), an epic Telugu-language action film. Most animals in the film were computer-generated.

supporting conservation efforts. In the USA, the U.S. Fish and Wildlife Service can take action to protect species in decline, as provided for in the Endangered Species Act of 1973, though it can be a laborious and slow process. After more than two decades of petitioning by advocates for the bird, the U.S. Fish and Wildlife Service declared the Western yellow-billed cuckoo (*Coccyzus americanus*) 'threatened' in 2014. These handsome birds pair up, build nests and care for young; when their favourite foods, including tent caterpillars, are abundant, they may lay enough to leave eggs in robin or catbird nests, too. Once found during breeding season along forested riverbanks from British Columbia in the north to northwestern Mexico to the south, their numbers have dropped dramatically. Now they are found much more rarely, mostly in California, Arizona and New Mexico. Not until 2021 did the Fish and Wildlife Service order the preservation of 'critical habitat' – almost 121,405 hectares (300,000 ac) of it – to help protect the yellow-billed cuckoo from threats including habitat loss and eggshell thinning caused by exposure to pesticides, among other factors.[19]

Animals like cuckoos survive in a complex web of predators and prey, parasites and hosts, native species and those that we have introduced or allowed to invade new parts of the world. They are also subject to a not-so-delicate and often destructive dance with the expansion of human culture. Our agriculture and dependence on agrochemicals, our extractive industries and our sprawling overdevelopment not only degrade or destroy natural habitats, squeezing fauna into smaller and more fragmented territories. Their enormous greenhouse-gas emissions, especially of carbon dioxide and methane, are warming the planet, reshaping bioclimatic zones and impacting food supplies and other conditions of habitability, as well as affecting the timing of annual migrations and breeding seasons.

Our brushes with wildlife of all kinds – common cuckoos included, those more-often-heard-than-seen seasonal visitors – which take place in and around the fringes of urban life remind us of a natural world that pre-dates the human footprint on this Earth. Thanks to those encounters, birdsong influences our musical compositions, we mark the passage of time, and we mine our myths and metaphors. What will fire our imaginations once we push these creatures further away, and into precarity? Our memories and artefacts will not be enough to sustain the already tenuous relationship between human culture and the very nature upon which we depend.

Timeline of the Cuckoo

60 MYA	20 MYA	c. 414 BCE	c. 350 BCE
The major groups of cuckoos are evolving distinctly	Fossils that can be identified with some certainty as cuckoos begin to form	*The Birds* by Aristophanes is performed for the first time in Athens. The play introduces the idea of 'Cloud Cuckoo Land'	In *The History of Animals*, Aristotle recognizes brood parasitism and tries to debunk the myth that the sparrowhawk transforms into the cuckoo for part of each year

1662	1716	c. 1730S	1739
The first of many poems by Matsuo Bashō is published; he goes on to become a prolific master of the haiku form, with many of his works featuring cuckoos	Antonio Vivaldi publishes his Violin Concerto in A major, known as 'The Cuckoo'	Clockmaking crafts-people in Germany's Black Forest create household clocks that contain a tiny carved bird and that make the call of the cuckoo on the hour	Handel writes the Organ Concerto in F Major, known as 'The Cuckoo and the Nightingale'

1917		1918–25	1922
Nora Barnacle begins a letter to her husband, James Joyce, with the salutation 'Dear Cuckold'		Oologist Edgar Percival Chance undertakes his groundbreaking studies of cuckoo breeding seasons at Wicken Fen, near Cambridge, UK	Joyce's *Ulysses*, which makes regular use of cuckoo-clocks and cuckold epithets, is published

77 CE	12TH–13TH CENTURY	1387–1400	c. 1589–1613
Pliny the Elder's *Natural History* covers much of the same material as Aristotle did, but mistakenly claims that a cuckoo kills and eats its foster-mother before fledging	*The Owl and the Nightingale*, a comic poem, contains the first known use of the term 'cuckold', derived from 'cuckoo'	Geoffrey Chaucer writes *The Canterbury Tales*. Cuckolded characters appear in 'The Miller's Tale' and 'The Wife of Bath's Tale'	William Shakespeare weaves symbolic cuckoos and purported cuckolds into many of his plays, including *Cymbeline, The Merry Wives of Windsor, Much Ado About Nothing, Othello, Troilus and Cressida* and *The Winter's Tale*

c. 1840	1859	1879	1886
Black Forest cuckoo-clockmaking is industrialized, employing half a million people on factory assembly lines	Charles Darwin, in *On the Origin of Species*, examines the cuckoo's instinct to lay her eggs in another bird's nest	James Hardy publishes his 'Popular History of the Cuckoo'	Camille Saint-Saëns writes 'The Cuckoo in the Depth of the Woods', a movement within his *Carnival of the Animals*

1922	1962	1990	2011
P. G. Wodehouse uses the word 'cuckoo' to mean 'a little crazy' in one of his Jeeves stories	A Madison Avenue advertising agency introduces Sonny the Cuckoo Bird, an animated mascot promoting the General Mills cereal Cocoa Puffs	The Cuckoo Clock (now Cuckooland) Museum is established in Tabley, Cheshire, UK	Researchers at BTO begin the Cuckoo Tracking Project, using satellite technology to gather data about the routes taken by migrating cuckoos

References

1 WHAT IS A CUCKOO?

1   This haiku is from Matsuo Bashō's poetry collection *The Seashell Game*, published in 1672 and quoted in Matsuo Bashō, *Bashō: The Complete Haiku*, ed. and trans. Jane Reichhold (Tokyo, 2008), pp. 23, 25.

2   Charles Darwin, *On the Origin of Species* [1859] (London, 2003), p. 255.

3   Ed Yong, 'Cuckoos Mimic Hawks to Fool Small Birds', *Discover*, www.discovermagazine.com, 7 May 2008.

4   James Hardy, 'Popular History of the Cuckoo', *Folk-Lore Record*, II/1 (1879), p. 47.

5   Bethan Roberts [@lloydbethanr], Twitter, https://twitter.com, 28 April 2023.

6   Aristotle, *The History of Animals*, trans. D'Arcy Wentworth Thompson, Book VI, Part 7 (Oxford, 1910), at https://penelope.uchicago.edu, accessed 2 August 2023.

7   Pliny the Elder, *The Natural History*, trans. John Bostock, Book X, Chap. 11 [London, 1855], at www.perseus.tufts.edu, accessed 3 August 2023.

8   Yong, 'Cuckoos Mimic Hawks'. See also N. B. Davies and J. A. Welbergen, 'Cuckoo-Hawk Mimicry? An Experimental Test', *Proceedings of the Royal Society B: Biological Sciences*, CCLXXV/1644 (7 August 2008), pp. 1817–22.

9   Clifford Stoll, *The Cuckoo's Egg: Tracking a Spy Through the Maze of Computer Espionage* (New York, 1989).

10 Robert B. Payne, *The Cuckoos* (Oxford, 2005), p. xix; Johannes

Erritzøe et al., *Cuckoos of the World* (London, 2012), p. 11. Both
volumes have been invaluable sources in the present work.

11 Payne, *The Cuckoos*, pp. 109–10.

12 Ibid., p. 111.

13 Ibid., p. 5.

14 Ibid., p. 43.

15 Ibid., p. 4.

16 Ibid., pp. 45–6.

17 W. L. McAtee, 'The Shedding of the Stomach Lining by
Birds, Particularly as Exemplified by the Anatidæ', *The Auk*,
XXXIV (1917), pp. 415–21; Michael J. Caduto, 'Of Cuckoos and
Caterpillars', *Northern Woodlands*, https://northernwoodlands.org,
10 July 2005.

18 'Banded Ground-Cuckoo', IUCN Red List of Threatened Species,
www.iucnredlist.org, accessed 5 August 2023.

19 Payne categorizes the malkohas in the genera *Rhinortha*,
Phaenicophaeus, *Rhamphococcyx*, *Dasylophus*, *Zanclostomus* and
Taccocua; see his *The Cuckoos*, p. xi. Erritzøe et al. add *Rhopodytes*
and *Lepidogrammas* and reorganize some of the others; see their
Cuckoos of the World, p. 6.

20 Innes Cuthill (Professor of Behavioural Ecology, University of
Bristol), email correspondence, 3 January 2022.

21 Karen Marchetti, Hiroshi Nakamura and H. Lisle Gibbs,
'Host-Race Formation in the Common Cuckoo', *Science*,
CCLXXXII/5388 (16 October 1998), pp. 471–2; H. Lisle Gibbs et al.,
'Genetic Evidence for Female Host-Specific Races of the Common
Cuckoo', *Nature*, CDVII/6801 (14 September 2000), pp. 183–6.

2 'DEAR CUCKOLD'

1 Alan Hughes and Gordon Zellaby discuss a sudden, inexplicable
baby boom in their village, in John Wyndham's *The Midwich
Cuckoos* (1957), p. 94.

2 Charles Darwin, *On the Origin of Species* [1859] (New York, 2003),
p. 244.

3   Ibid., p. 253.
4   Ibid., p. 255.
5   Aesop, 'Fable 393: The Cuckoo, the Hedge-Sparrow, and the Owl',
    Aesop's Fables, adapted by William C. Michael [2022], at
    https://classicalliberalarts.com, accessed 6 August 2023.
6   John Gerard and Thomas Johnson, 'Of Wild Water-Cresses, or
    Cuckoo-flowers', in *The Herbal, or General History of Plants*, rev. and
    expanded edn, Book II, Part 1 [1633], at https://exclassics.com,
    accessed 30 July 2023.
7   Green's Dictionary of Slang cites use of the words 'cuckoo' and
    'cuckoo's nest' to refer to sex organs from *c*. 1800, but 'cuckoo pint'
    and 'cuckoo flower' were already common English-language names
    for these plants. See https://greensdictofslang.com, accessed
    30 July 2023.
8   The first use of 'cuckquean' in print seems to be in John Heywood,
    The Proverbs and Epigrams of John Heywood (London, 1867),
    reprinted from a 1562 volume.
9   *The Owl and the Nightingale*, trans. Simon Armitage (Princeton, NJ,
    2022), p. 107.
10 Mark I. Millington and Alison S. Sinclair, 'The Honourable Cuckold:
    Models of Masculine Defence', *Comparative Literature Studies*,
    XXIX/2 (1992), p. 3. See also Geoffrey Chaucer, *The Canterbury Tales*,
    trans. Nevill Coghill (London and New York, 2003).
11 Millington and Sinclair, 'The Honourable Cuckold', p. 1.
12 Ibid.; the authors explore this theme in the Federico García Lorca
    play *Amor de don Perlimplín con Belisa en su jardín* (1933) and the
    novel *Before She Met Me* by Julian Barnes (1982).
13 Ibid., p. 2.
14 Ibid., emphasis added.
15 Stephen Cohen, '"No Assembly but Horn Beasts": The Politics of
    Cuckoldry in Shakespeare's Romantic Comedies', *Journal for Early
    Modern Cultural Studies*, IV/2 (2004), p. 6.
16 Christina León Alfar, *Women and Shakespeare's Cuckoldry Plays:
    Shifting Narratives of Marital Betrayal* (Oxford and New York,
    2017), p. viii.

17 For more on the cuckoo and cuckolds in Shakespeare, a good place to start is Missy Dunaway, 'Birds of Shakespeare: The Cuckoo', *Folger Shakespeare Library*, www.folger.edu/blogs, 17 May 2022.

18 Claire McEachern, 'Why Do Cuckolds Have Horns?', *Huntington Library Quarterly*, LXXI/4 (2008), p. 610.

19 C. J. Cherryh, *Cuckoo's Egg* (New York, 1985).

20 John Wyndham, *The Midwich Cuckoos* (London, 2008), p. 111.

21 Ibid., p. 156.

22 Brenda Maddox, *Nora: The Real Life of Molly Bloom* (New York, 1988), pp. 115–16.

23 Ibid., p. 149.

24 See James Joyce, *Ulysses*, foreword Morris L. Ernst (New York, 1990), especially Episode 4: Calypso, Episode 9: Scylla and Charybdis and Episode 18: Penelope.

25 Ibid., p. 470.

26 Ibid., pp. 382, 469.

27 Ibid., p. 212.

28 Alexandra Minna Stern, *Proud Boys and the White Ethnostate: How the Alt-Right Is Warping the American Imagination* (Boston, MA, 2019), p. 73.

29 Alind Chauhan, 'Musk Calls Zuckerberg a "Cuck": The Story of the Far-Right's Favorite Insult', *Indian Express*, https://indianexpress.com, 11 July 2023.

30 Joyce, *Ulysses*, p. 212.

31 Ibid., p. 213.

3 MYTH AND MADNESS

1 P. G. Wodehouse's 'Bingo and the Little Woman' was first published in an issue of *Strand* in the UK (November 1922) and *Cosmopolitan* in the USA (December 1922).

2 Aesop, 'Fable 364: The Bee and the Cuckoo', *Aesop's Fables*, adapted by William C. Michael [2022], at https://classicalliberalarts.com, accessed 20 July 2023.

3   Theocritus, *Idyll xx: Town and Country*, trans. Charles Stuart
    Calverley [1869], at www.gutenberg.org, accessed 11 October 2023.

4   Jennifer Neville, 'Fostering the Cuckoo: "Exeter Book" Riddle 9',
    Review of English Studies, LVIII/236 (2007), p. 432.

5   Ibid., p. 436.

6   Ibid., p. 442.

7   C. M. Lai, 'Messenger of Spring and Morality: Cuckoo Lore in
    Chinese Sources', *Journal of the American Oriental Society*, CXVIII/4
    (1998), pp. 530–31. In addition to some variant spellings of these
    words for cuckoo, Lai also offers *daisheng*, but notes that this term
    probably actually references the hoopoe, resulting from some
    confusion about which bird is which.

8   Ibid., pp. 531, 534.

9   Ibid., p. 537.

10 Ngawang Phuntsho, *The Cuckoo and the Pigeon*, ebook (Varanasi,
    India, 2009).

11 Avatar Vani, 'Goodness is Godliness', in *Sanathana Sarathi:
    The Eternal Charioteer: Collection of Volumes from 1990–1999* [2022],
    at https://books.google.com, accessed 26 July 2023.

12 Fanny Hagin Mayer, ed., trans., *The Yanagita Kunio Guide to the
    Japanese Folktale* (Tokyo, 1948), unpag. reprint. Folktale No. 269 in
    Chapter 16. Takes about Burds, Beasts, Plants and Trees. See
    https://publish.iupress.indiana.edu.

13 'Summer 1681: no. 53', Matsuo Bashō, 'Basho's Haiku: Selected
    Poems of Matsuo Bashō', trans. David Landis Barnhill (Albany,
    NY, 2004), p. 28.

14 Ichiro Hori, 'Mountains and Their Importance for the Idea of the
    Other World in Japanese Folk Religion', *History of Religions*, VI/1
    (August 1966), p. 11.

15 The rhyme quoted is a version that Hardy notes was common in
    Gloucester. He harvested these lines from an earlier compendium:
    see William Howitt, *The Book of the Seasons; or, The Calendar of
    Nature* (London, 1831).

16 Lammas Tide, or Lammas Day, is a Christian celebration of the early
    harvest on 1 August. Hardy took this rhyme from Jean L. Watson's

Round the Grange Farm: or, Good Old Times (London, 1876), cited in James Hardy, 'Popular History of the Cuckoo', *Folk-Lore Record*, ɪɪ/1 (1879), p. 20.

17 Hardy, 'Popular History of the Cuckoo', p. 53.

18 Ibid., pp. 56–7, 69, 72, 88–9, 91.

19 Mark Cocker and David Tipling, *Birds and People* (London, 2013), p. 267.

20 Hardy, 'Popular History of the Cuckoo', p. 89.

21 Thomas McKay, 'Hunt the Gowk: The History of April Fool's in Scotland and Why Its [*sic*] Known as Huntigowk Day', *The Scotsman*, 31 March 2023.

22 Aristophanes, *The Birds*, trans. Anon. (Auckland, 2010), p. 41.

23 Ibid., p. 42.

24 Vivian Shaw (Gilbert Seldes), 'The Cuckoo School of Humour in America', *Vanity Fair* (May 1924), cited and partially reproduced in Rob King, *Hokum! The Early Sound Slapstick Short and Depression-Era Mass Culture* (Berkeley, CA, 2017). See especially pp. 21–5.

25 Jackson R. Bryer, '"Better That All of the Story Never Be Told": Zelda Fitzgerald's Sister's Letters to Arthur Mizener', *F. Scott Fitzgerald Review*, xxv/1 (2017), p. 442.

26 Ken Kesey, *One Flew Over the Cuckoo's Nest* (New York, 2003), pp. 50–51. Kesey's novel was adapted for the Broadway stage by Dale Wasserman, starring Kirk Douglas as McMurphy (1963). The play was the basis of the acclaimed film directed by Miloš Forman (1975) with Jack Nicholson as McMurphy and Louise Fletcher as Ratched.

27 Ibid., p. 246.

28 In a review essay, the poet George Scarbrough used the rhyme and the game (which recalls the simpler 'duck, duck, goose' game of my childhood) to frame the body of work he was exploring as a soaring, strapping, sprawling hodge-podge ('American poetry is a cuckoo's nest!'), which he meant largely as a compliment. See George Scarbrough, 'Review: One Flew East, One Flew West, One Flew Over the Cuckoo's Nest', *Sewanee Review*, LXXI/1 (Winter 1965), pp. 138–9. Nowhere does he mention Kesey's novel.

29 John Nichols, *The Sterile Cuckoo* (New York, 1965), pp. 185–6.

30 Commercials Ads, 'Cocoa Puffs Commercials Compilation Cuckoo Bird', available at www.youtube.com, *c.* 2018, accessed 26 July 2023.

31 Hardy, 'Popular History of the Cuckoo', p. 72.

32 Gerald Durrell, *The Drunken Forest* (Harmondsworth, 1958), p. 25.

33 Ibid., p. 27.

34 Ibid., p. 28.

35 Ibid., pp. 28–9.

36 The curious stands of tall trees on raised ground that Field found from Wales to Oxford and beyond are more likely defensive artefacts of the conflicts between Britons and Saxons after Rome abandoned the British Isles than any attempt to pen the cuckoo.

37 John Edward Field, *The Myth of the Pent Cuckoo: A Study in Folklore* (London, 1913), p. 1.

38 Ibid., p. 48.

4 NATURE'S TIMEKEEPER

1 This epigraph is from Greene's screenplay for the canonical film noir *The Third Man* (1949), but the line may have been improvised by actor Orson Welles. The confusion was common. After the First World War, clocks and other products manufactured in Germany were often exported out of Switzerland to mask their country of origin. See Jack Tempest, 'World's Largest Collection of Cuckoo Clocks', *Antiques and Collecting Magazine*, XCIX/9 (November 1994), p. 4.

2 William Wordsworth, 'To the Cuckoo', in *Poems in Two Volumes* (London, 1807).

3 R. Lydekker, 'On Hearing the First Cuckoo', in *The First Cuckoo: Letters to The Times, 1900–1980*, ed. Kenneth Gregory, 2nd edn (London, 1981), p. 83.

4 David Mallon, 'Their First Cuckoo?', in Gregory, *The First Cuckoo*, pp. 316–17. Mallon's letter was published 25 June 1977.

5 Chris Hewson (Senior Research Ecologist, British Trust for Ornithology), email correspondence, 6 July 2023.

6   As if the honour of publishing a letter in *The Times* of London were not reward enough, anyone hearing the first cuckoo to return to the UK in 2015 might have earned a more fungible prize. In a stunt designed to raise awareness of the declining cuckoo population, the BTO and the gambling enterprise William Hill launched 'The Great Cuckoo Race' as an opportunity to bet on which tagged bird would be the first springtime arrival. See Hannah Keyser, 'British Gamblers Bet on Cuckoo Migration', *Mental Floss*, www.mentalfloss.com, 4 May 2015; Stuart Winter, 'Returning to Britain: Epic Flight of the Cuckoo Begins . . . And You Can Bet on the Race', *Daily Express*, www.express.co.uk, 3 April 2015.

7   Paul Stancliffe, 'Celebrating PJ', *British Trust for Ornithology*, www.bto.org, accessed 11 July 2023.

8   'Cuckoo 5', *The Mongolia Cuckoo Project*, https://birdingbeijing. com/the-mongolia-cuckoo-project, 15 October 2020.

9   'Farewell to Charles', *British Trust for Ornithology*, www.bto.org, 28 June 2022.

10   I was fortunate enough to hear two cuckoos, the first on 4 June 2023 on the outskirts of Wivenhoe, a small town in Essex, calling from a thicket grown up around the train tracks. The second called repeatedly just to the south, stopping me in my tracks on a path fringed on one side by woods and on the other by Colne River in Alresford.

11   Karl Kochmann, *Black Forest Clockmaker and the Cuckoo Clock*, 7th edn (Concord, CA, 1992), p. 4.

12   Ibid., pp. 50, 57, 102.

13   Jefferson's 'Great Clock', which he designed himself, ran on a system of weighted chains – and those weights were extra-large, at 8 kilograms (18 lb) each, in the shape of cannonballs rather than pine cones. Unfortunately, the clock had no cuckoo. See 'Great Clock', *Thomas Jefferson's Monticello*, www.monticello.org, accessed 24 July 2023.

14   Peter Henault, 'Black Forest Cuckoo Clocks', *German Life*, 1/1 (31 July 1994).

15 'Das Bahnhäusle – ein Jahrhundertdesign aus Furtwangen (Teil 2)'
    ('The Train House – A Design of the Century from Furtwagen,
    Part 2'), blog, Deutsches Uhrenmuseum, https://
    blog.deutsches-uhrenmuseum.de, 3 August 2017.

16 Philip Shabecoff, 'Cuckoo Clocks Show a Decline', *New York Times*
    (24 August 1965), p. 46.

17 'Tick-Tack-Quiz', *Das Fernsehlexikon* (The Television Dictionary),
    www.fernsehlexikon.de, accessed 11 October 2023.

18 Marianne Rohrlich, 'Deconstructing the Cuckoo', *New York Times*
    (18 December 1997), p. F8.

19 Tempest, 'World's Largest Collection', p. 4.

20 'List of Largest Cuckoo Clocks', https://en.wikipedia.org, accessed
    11 July 2023; Anwesha Ray, 'The Most Famous Cuckoo Clocks in
    Germany', https://theculturetrip.com, 27 July 2018; 'The World's
    Largest Cuckoo Clock', https://visitsugarcreek.com, accessed
    11 July 2023.

21 The phrase is repeated throughout the story. See Mary Louisa
    Molesworth, *The Cuckoo Clock* (London, 1877), p. 11; www.
    gutenberg.org, accessed 11 October 2023.

22 Ellis Bell (Emily Brontë), *Wuthering Heights* (New York, 1858), p. 31.

23 Ibid., p. 213.

24 Mathias Malzieu, *The Boy with the Cuckoo-Clock Heart*, trans. Sarah
    Ardizzone (New York, 2009), p. 8. First published as *La Mécanique
    du Coeur* (Paris, 2007). Malzieu's band Dionysos released an
    album of the same name in 2007. An animated film version,
    Jack et la mécanique du coeur, was released in 2013 with the band's
    music as soundtrack; the 2014 English-language version is *Jack
    and the Cuckoo-Clock Heart*.

25 Kiyotaka Akasaka, 'Cuckoo Watch', at https://hackaday.io,
    accessed 11 July 2023.

26 The clock that belonged to my father closely resembles a model
    manufactured by Anton Schneider GmbH & Co., which has been
    operating in Schonach, Germany, since 1848. See Rohrlich,
    'Deconstructing the Cuckoo', p. F8.

1   Margaret A. Barrett, 'Correspondence: The Cuckoo's Notes',
    The Musical Times (1 October 1987), p. 697, citing *Transactions
    of the Linnean Society*, vol. VII (1804), p. 310. Most sources say
    that the cuckoo typically sings in the key of C (see 'Cuckoo',
    Los Doggies, www.losdoggies.com, 8 November 2016). Barrett
    notes that D, D sharp or D flat have also been heard, citing
    Gilbert White, 'Letter XLV', in *The Natural History and Antiquities
    of Selbourne* (London, 1789), p. 127.

2   John S. Farmer, ed., *The Proverbs, Epigrams, and Miscellanies
    of John Heywood* (London, 1906), p. 294.

3   Csaba Moskát and Mark E. Hauber, 'Male Common Cuckoos
    Use a Three-Note Variant of the "Cu-Coo" Call for Duetting with
    Conspecific Females', *Behavioural Process*, CXCI (October 2021).

4   White, *The Natural History*, p. 382.

5   Clare Stares, quoted in Mark Cocker, *Birds and People*
    (New York, 2014), p. 264.

6   For 'bubbling', Edgar Percival Chance, *The Truth About the Cuckoo*
    (London, 1940); Yanyi Want et al., 'Testing the Interspecific
    Function of the Female Common Cuckoo "Bubbling" Call',
    Frontiers in Ecological Evolution, IX (2021). For a 'chuckle', see
    Jenny E. York and Nicholas B. Davies, 'Female Cuckoo Calls
    Misdirect Host Defences towards the Wrong Enemy', *Nature
    Ecology and Evolution*, 1/10 (2017), pp. 1520–25. For 'gurgling',
    see David Attenborough, 'Tweet of the Day: Cuckoo – Female',
    www.bbc.co.uk/sounds, 31 May 2013; 'Tweet Take 5: The
    Cuckoo', www.bbc.co.uk/sounds, 4 April 2021.

7   'Common Cuckoo: Sounds and Calls', https://wildambience.com,
    accessed 7 July 2023. This webpage includes a link to a video that
    has on its audio track both male and female cuckoo sounds.

8   Chance, *The Truth About the Cuckoo*, p. 26.

9   Ibid., p. 22.

10 Paul Dinning, 'Sparrowhawk Call – What Sound Do Sparrowhawks
    Make? – Birds of Prey', available at www.youtube.com,
    16 August 2015.

11   York and Davies, 'Female Cuckoo Calls'. See also 'Cuckoo Call
     Adds Another Layer of Deception ', *Nature*, 549 (7 September
     2017), p. 6.

12   'Cuckoo Calling', p. 6.

13   George Dvorsky, 'Cuckoos Are Even Bigger Assholes Than
     We Realized', https://gizmodo.com, 5 September 2017.

14   The Cornell Lab of Ornithology website is a wonderful place
     to listen to recorded birdsong, simply by searching for any
     species and clicking on 'Sounds'. Cornell Lab of Ornithology,
     www.allaboutbirds.org, accessed 26 July 2023.

15   Enam Ul Haque, 'Common Hawk-Cuckoo: An Uncommon
     Impersonator and an Amazing Vocalist', *Business Standard*,
     www.tbsnews.net, 18 June 2022.

16   See Bethan Roberts, *Nightingale* (London, 2021).

17   Timothy Judd, 'Mahler and the Cuckoo', https://thelistenersclub.
     com, 18 April 2018.

18   For another reading, see Jessica Duchen, 'A Guide to Saint-Saëns's
     Carnival of the Animals, the Animals Represented and Its Best
     Recordings', *BBC Music Magazine*, www.classical-music.com,
     22 July 2021.

19   On the critics' squabbles, see Owen Jander, 'The Prophetic
     Conversation in Beethoven's "Scene by the Brook"', *Musical
     Quarterly*, LXXVII/3 (1993), pp. 508–59.

20   Ibid.

21   James Hardy, 'Popular History of the Cuckoo', *Folk-Lore Record*,
     II/1 (1879), pp. 47–50, drawing on William Howitt, *The Book of
     the Seasons; or, the Calendar of Nature* (London, 1831). For the
     broadsheets, search for Roud number 413 at *Broadside Ballads
     Online from the Bodleian Libraries*, http://ballads.bodleian.ox.ac.uk.

22   Unfortunately, given strict copyright rules involving lyrics, I can't
     quote the song, but interested readers will be able to find it easily.

23   John Batchelor, *Bird Cults of the Ainu of Japan* [1901?], ebook.

1 George Scarbrough, 'Review: One Flew East, One Flew West, One Flew Over the Cuckoo's Nest', *Sewanee Review*, LXXI/1 (Winter 1965).

2 Search cuckoo species by common or Latin name at the BirdLife International DataZone (http://datazone.birdlife.org) or at the IUCN Red List of Threatened Species (www.iucnredlist.org).

3 'Common Cuckoo *Cuculus canorus*', http://datazone.birdlife.org, accessed 6 August 2023.

4 J.J.N. Heywood et al., *The Breeding Bird Survey 2022*, British Trust for Ornithology (Thetford, UK, 2023), pp. 17, 19.

5 Chris M. Hewson et al., 'Population Decline Is Linked to Migration Route in the Common Cuckoo', *Nature Communications*, VII/12296 (2016).

6 Edgar Percival Chance tracked cuckoos as they laid eggs throughout several seasons in Wicken Fen, proudly recording that one such 'remarkable bird' laid 25 eggs in May and June 1922, 'a continuous and unbroken sequence never likely to be equalled so long as cuckoos continue to lay!' Edgar Percival Chance, *The Truth About the Cuckoo* (London, 1940), p. 96.

7 A. P. Moller et al., 'Rapid Change in Host Use of the Common Cuckoo *Cuculus canorus* Linked to Climate Change', *Royal Publishing Society Proceedings Biol. Sci.*, CCLXXVIII/1706 (7 March 2011), pp. 733–8.

8 Heywood et al., *The Breeding Bird Survey 2022*, p. 17.

9 Vladimir Dinets et al., 'Predicting the Responses of Native Birds to Transoceanic Invasions by Avian Brood Parasites', *Journal of Field Ornithology*, LXXXVI/3 (2015), p. 245; Vladimir Dinets et al., 'Striking Difference in Response to Expanding Brood Parasites by Birds in Western and Eastern Beringia', *Journal of Field Ornithology*, LXXXIX/2 (2018), p. 117.

10 Dinets et al., 'Predicting the Responses', pp. 245, 247–9.

11 Ibid., p. 247.

12 An essential source for up-to-date information on animal populations is the IUCN's Red List of Threatened Species,

which designates species as 'not evaluated', 'data deficient',
'least concern', 'near threatened', 'vulnerable', 'endangered',
'critically endangered', 'extinct in the wild' and 'extinct'; see
www.iucnredlist.org. Another excellent source is the website
of species-by-species status reports from BirdLife International:
see http://datazone.birdlife.org.

13 'Snail-eating Coua *Coua delalandei*', http://datazone.birdlife.org,
accessed 4 August 2023.

14 Johannes Erritzøe et al., *Cuckoos of the World* (London, 2012),
p. 227 says none were collected after 1834; Robert B. Payne,
The Cuckoos (Oxford, 2005), pp. 280–81 gives 1850 as the date the
last specimen was collected.

15 'Red-Crested Malkoha *Phaenicophaeus pyrrhocephalus*',
http://datazone.birdlife.org, accessed 4 August 2023.

16 'Coral-Billed Ground-Cuckoo *Carpococcyx renauldi*',
http://datazone.birdlife.org, accessed 4 August 2023.

17 'Bornean Ground-Cuckoo *Carpococcyx radiceus*',
http://datazone.birdlife.org, accessed 4 August 2023.

18 'Bay-Breasted Cuckoo *Coccyzus rufigularis*', http://datazone.
birdlife.org, accessed 4 August 2023. This species is identified
as *Hyetornis rufigularis* in Erritzøe et al., *Cuckoos of the World*,
pp. 310–11.

19 See 'Endangered and Threatened Wildlife and Plants;
Determination of Threatened Status for the Western Distinct
Population Segment of the Yellow-Billed Cuckoo (*Coccyzus
americanus*)', www.federalregister.gov, 3 October 2014,
pp. 59991–60038; 'Endangered and Threatened Wildlife
and Plants; Designation of Critical Habitat for the Western
Distinct Population Segment of the Yellow-Billed Cuckoo',
www.federalregister.gov, 21 April 2021, pp. 20798–1005;
Sonya Daw, 'Western Yellow-Billed Cuckoo', www.nps.gov,
November 2014, accessed 4 August 2023; and 'Yellow-Billed
Cuckoo', www.biologicaldiversity.org, accessed 5 August 2023.

Select Bibliography

Aristophanes, *The Birds*, trans. Anon. (Auckland, 2010)

Aristotle, *The History of Animals*, trans. D'Arcy Wentworth Thompson, Book VI, Part 7 (Oxford, 1910)

Birkhead, Tim, *The Most Perfect Thing: Inside (and Outside) a Bird's Egg* (New York, 2016)

Chance, Edgar Percival, *The Cuckoo's Secret* (London, 1922)

—, *The Truth About the Cuckoo* (London, 1940)

Cocker, Mark, and David Tipling, *Birds and People* (London, 2013)

Darwin, Charles, *On the Origin of Species* (New York, 2003)

Davies, Nick, *Cuckoo: Cheating by Nature* (New York, 2015)

—, *Cuckoos, Cowbirds and Other Cheats* (London, 2000)

Doerr, Anthony, *Cloud Cuckoo Land* (New York, 2021)

Erritzøe, Johannes, et al., *Cuckoos of the World* (London, 2012)

Field, John Edward, *The Myth of the Pent Cuckoo: A Study in Folklore* (London, 1913)

Hardy, James, 'Popular History of the Cuckoo', *Folk-Lore Record*, II/1 (1879), pp. 47–91

Healy, Tim, 'A Tale of Two Cuckoos,' *Nemesis Bird*, https://nemesisbird.com/birding/tale-two-cuckoos, 11 November 2020

Heywood, J.J.N., et al., *The Breeding Bird Survey 2022*, British Trust for Ornithology (Thetford, UK, 2023)

Hogben, John, 'The Birds of Wordsworth', *Gentleman's Magazine*, CCLXXXIV/2020 (June 1898), pp. 532–40

Joyce, James, *Ulysses* (New York, 1990)

McCarthy, Michael, *Say Goodbye to the Cuckoo: Migratory Birds and the Impending Ecological Catastrophe* (Chicago, IL, 2010)

Maddox, Brenda, *Nora: The Real Life of Molly Bloom* (New York, 1988)

Malzieu, Mathias, *The Boy with the Cuckoo-Clock Heart*, trans. Sarah Ardizzone (New York, 2009)

Mikulica, Oldřich, et al., *The Cuckoo: The Uninvited Guest* (Plymouth, 2017)

Millington, Mark I., and Alison S. Sinclair, 'The Honourable Cuckold: Models of Masculine Defence', *Comparative Literature Studies*, XXIX/1 (1992), pp. 1–19

Morelli, Federico, et al., 'The Common Cuckoo Is an Effective Indicator of High Bird Species Richness in Asia and Europe', *Nature: Scientific Reports*, VII/4376 (2017)

Payne, Robert B., *The Cuckoos* (Oxford, 2005)

Rey, Eugene, *Old and New Information Concerning the Domestic Economy of the Cuckoo* (Leipzig, 1892)

White, Gilbert, *The Natural History and Antiquities of Selbourne* (London, 1789)

Wyllie, Ian, *The Cuckoo* (New York, 1981)

Associations and Websites

AFRICAN CUCKOOS: RESEARCH ON BROOD PARASITES
AND OTHER CURIOUS AFRICAN BIRDS
Department of Zoology, University of Cambridge, UK, and FitzPatrick
Institute of African Ornithology, University of Cape Town, South Africa
www.africancuckoos.com

THE BEIJING CUCKOO PROJECT
https://birdingbeijing.com/beijing-cuckoo-project

THE BIRDS OF SHAKESPEARE
Missy Dunaway Creative Studios
www.birdsofshakespeare.com

CUCKOO TRACKING PROJECT
British Trust for Ornithology
The Nunnery
Thetford, Norfolk
IP24 2PU, UK
www.bto.org/our-science/projects/cuckoo-tracking-project

DATA ZONE
BirdLife International
http://datazone.birdlife.org

GERMAN CLOCK MUSEUM (DEUTSCHES UHRENMUSEUM)
Robert-Gerwig-Platz 1

78120 Furtwangen im Schwarzwald, Germany
www.deutsches-uhrenmuseum.de/no_cache/start.html

INTERNATIONAL UNION FOR CONSERVATION OF NATURE
www.iucnredlist.org

JAMES J. FIORENTINO FOUNDATION AND MUSEUM
126 North 1st Street
Minneapolis, MN 55401, USA
https://fiorentinomuseum.org

THE MONGOLIA CUCKOO PROJECT
https://birdingbeijing.com/the-mongolia-cuckoo-project

ROYAL SOCIETY FOR THE PROTECTION OF BIRDS
The Lodge, Potton Road
Sandy, Bedfordshire
SG19 2DL, UK
WWW.RSPB.ORG.UK

Media

'Cuckoo', *David Attenborough's Life Stories*, BBC Radio 4 Extra, 20 May 2011, www.bbc.co.uk/sounds

'Cuckoo!', *Natural World*, narr. David Attenborough, BBC 2, 9 January 2009

'Cuckoo', *Rhythms of Nature in the Barycz Valley* [Poland], Saturnina and Artur Homan, 2013, www.youtube.com

The Cuckoo's Secret, prod. Edgar Percival Chance, British Instructional Films, 1922

Acknowledgements

A book is never just the work of one person, but rather a conversation among many individuals and myriad texts. *Cuckoo* is no exception. In my previous contribution to Reaktion's Animal series, *Crab* (2021), I called myself a 'curious outsider', diving into worlds of marine biology and crustacean-inspired culture that were both fascinating and welcoming. The same holds true here, as my encounters with the cuckoo literature, ornithological research, the sometimes 'cuckoo' stories that have been told about these wonderful birds – and an occasional actual cuckoo – were full of surprises. I am grateful to everyone at Reaktion who made this opportunity possible: among them series editor Jonathan Burt, publisher Michael Leaman, Alex Ciobanu, assistant to the publisher, and Amy Salter, editor.

I also owe a debt of gratitude to the artists, photographers, collectors and organizations who granted permission for their works to be reproduced in this volume, including Graham Arader and Taylor Nash of Arader Galleries, John Caddick, John Combe of Wordsworth Grasmere, Cosmo Sheldrake, Michael Stubblefield, Jeff Sykes, Flora Wallace and Pete Walkden. Kudos, too, to the many museums, libraries and individual photographers who provide access to images in the public domain or under Creative Commons licences; they are doing invaluable service to support shared knowledge and visual culture. Likewise, scientists whom I have peppered with questions have been extremely helpful: Innes Cuthill, Professor of Behavioural Ecology, University of Bristol; Mark E. Hauber, Executive Director, Advanced Science Research Center, The Graduate Center of the City University of New York; Chris Hewson, Senior Research Ecologist, British Trust for Ornithology; and Paul R.

Sweet, Collection Manager, Department of Ornithology, American Museum of Natural History.

My thanks also go to the City University of New York's Research Foundation, whose Department Chair Research Accounts helped support this project. My warmest thanks to Miriam Glucksmann, Mark Harvey, Jeremy Krikler, Gary Phillips and Liz Snyder, who made sure that I heard cuckoos and the music around them. Ellen Brinks, Chris Gibson, Jude Gibson, Ishwari L. Keller, Andy Luck, Gerry Milligan, Deb Lawler Sharp and Kay Turner all pointed me to cuckoos I might have otherwise missed. Finally, to Arlene Stein, who walks many miles with me and reads every word I write, even when they are . . . a little bit cuckoo.

Photo Acknowledgements

The author and publishers wish to thank the organizations and individuals listed below for authorizing reproduction of their work.

Alamy: p. 34 (blickwinkel); courtesy of Graham Arader, Arader Galleries, Philadelphia: p. 30; Art Institute of Chicago: pp. 28 (Clarence Buckingham Collection), 46 (purchased with funds provided by Miss Louise Lutz), 48 (gift of Mr and Mrs Carter H. Harrison), 125 (Clarence Buckingham Collection); British Museum: p. 37 (public domain); Brooklyn Museum: p. 110 (gift of the Estate of Dr Eleanor Z. Wallace); John Caddick: pp. 17, 21; Cleveland Museum of Art: p. 62 (bequest of Edward L. Whittlemore); Cynthia Chris: pp. 13, 23 (American Museum of Natural History, Department of Ornithology), 24 (American Museum of Natural History, Department of Ornithology), 69, 101 left and right, 104, 117 (from author's collection), 118, 123 (from author's collection), 129; Dreamstime: pp. 12 (Vladimir Gnedin), 15 (DejaVu Designs), 18 (Mohd Hafez Abu Bakar), 22 (Girish Talwalkar), 31 (Wirestock), 52 (Howardkearley), 59 (Ephotocorp), 60 (Tatsuya Otsuka), 94 top (Jacqueline Nix), 109 (Ondřej Prosický); Flickr: pp. 10 (Caroline Legg/ CC BY 2.0), 56 (Carole Raddato/CC-BY-SA 2.0); Folger Shakespeare Library, Digital Image Collection: p. 88; Getty Museum Collection: p. 78 (public domain); Mario Gomes Collection: p. 91; Annie Harnett: p. 126 left; Sharon W. Houk/Phoenix Stage Company: p. 68; Lynn Hudson: p. 107; *Jack and the Cuckoo-Clock Heart* (2013): p. 99 (dir. Stéphane Berla and Mathias Malzieu/Production Companies: Duran, EuropaCorp, France 3 Cinema, uFilm, Walking the Dog); Library of Congress, Washington, DC: pp. 50, 90, 108, 111, 114, 130; Los Angeles County Museum of Art: p. 47 (gift of Allan and Maxine Kurtzman/

Index

Page numbers in *italics* refer to illustrations